Nurture

THIS STUDENT JOURNAL BELONGS TO:

NAME **Emily Griffin.**

CLASS **1ST Year.**

TEACHER **Ms. Hopkins.**

INTRODUCTION

In '**Nurture – A Student's Guide to Wellbeing Year One**' we have created a place for you to explore and develop your own wellbeing.

We are excited to be sharing this programme with you, which will enable you to manage your time efficiently, help you achieve peak performance in the classroom and gain high levels of student learning.

All Student Journal entries include Learning Goals and Statements of Learning, which show you what the lesson entails and what you will learn.

We incorporate the 8 Key Skills:

- being creative
- being literate
- being numerate
- communicating
- managing information & thinking
- staying well
- working with others

You will see icons in your Student Journal to show you which Wellbeing Indicators are being covered in each lesson and icons are also used to explain which tasks you are being asked to complete.

You'll discover that the Student Journal '**Nurture – A Student's Guide to Wellbeing Year One**' is packed full of activities and homework assignments to support your learning. We have utilised these exercises with our own students in our own classrooms with great success. We also hope you enjoy this programme and experience hugely positive and far-reaching effects on your wellbeing.

Good luck!

Team Nurture

Sanchia Connolly, Aran O'Driscoll and Holly Peters

First published 2019.

Second edition.

© 2020 Nurture4Wellbeing

www.nurture4wellbeing.com

ISBN: 9798648721609

CONTENTS

LESSON 1 - SETTING MYSELF UP IN MY NEW SCHOOL

DATE _____

LEARNING GOALS

At the conclusion of this activity, I will be able to;

- Identify key ways in which to get set up in my new school
- Demonstrate knowledge of lockers and timetable
- Evaluate understanding of locker organisation

JOURNAL ACTIVITY: (A) QUESTIONS

1. List 3 ways you can get yourself set up in your new school.

    → _____

    → _____

    → _____

2. When will you get your locker?

_____

3. Who is in charge of lockers?

_____

4. What do you do if you lose your key / forget your combination?

_____

_____

5. How should your books and copies be organised inside your locker?

_____

_____

6. What should be on the inside of your locker door?

_____

JOURNAL ACTIVITY: (B) THINK, PAIR, SHARE

Explain any 3 codes / abbreviations on your timetable.

→ _____

→ _____

→ _____

JOURNAL ACTIVITY: (C) TO-DO LIST

What's on your To-do List for the next lesson?

→ _____

→ _____

→ _____

→ _____

→ _____

→ _____

→ _____

LESSON REVIEW

3-2-1

3 THINGS I LEARNED TODAY

_____

_____

_____

2 THINGS I WILL CHANGE/IMPROVE

_____

_____

1 THING I WANT TO KNOW MORE ABOUT

_____

TRAFFIC LIGHTS

COLOUR THE TRAFFIC LIGHT WHICH BEST REPRESENTS YOUR UNDERSTANDING IN TODAY'S LESSON

Red: I don't understand at all and need help

Orange: I need some support and don't fully understand some aspects of what we learned about

Green: I am happy that I understand this lesson very well

INDICATORS OF WELLBEING

TICK THE BOX TO SHOW THE INDICATORS OF WELLBEING YOU IDENTIFY IN TODAY'S LESSON

LESSON 2 - WHO DO I GO TO FOR HELP?

LEARNING GOALS

At the conclusion of this activity, I will be able to;

- Identify key support personnel in my new school
- Demonstrate knowledge of the locations of these key people
- Evaluate understanding of possible situations in which to access the support structures available to me

JOURNAL ACTIVITY: (A) WHAT DO I DO IF?

As you are listening to your teacher, jot down any relevant names and places that you might need to remember in case of the following situations:

SITUATION	TEACHER / PERSON	CLASSROOM / PLACE
I have to leave school early...		
I have a note because I was sick...		
I am too sick to go to /stay in class...		
I have lost my keys...		
I am looking for my class teacher...		
I am upset / worried...		

JOURNAL ACTIVITY: (B) MY SCHOOL PASTORAL CARE STRUCTURE

Input the names of key personnel in the Pastoral Care Structure of your school in the boxes.

[ ] [ ] [ ] [ ]

[ ] [ ] [ ] [ ]

LESSON REVIEW

3-2-1

3 THINGS I LEARNED TODAY

_____

_____

_____

2 THINGS I WILL CHANGE/IMPROVE

_____

_____

1 THING I WANT TO KNOW MORE ABOUT

_____

TRAFFIC LIGHTS

COLOUR THE TRAFFIC LIGHT WHICH BEST REPRESENTS YOUR UNDERSTANDING IN TODAY'S LESSON

Red: I don't understand at all and need help

Orange: I need some support and don't fully understand some aspects of what we learned about

Green: I am happy that I understand this lesson very well

INDICATORS OF WELLBEING

TICK THE BOX TO SHOW THE INDICATORS OF WELLBEING YOU IDENTIFY IN TODAY'S LESSON

LESSON 3 - WELLBEING INDICATORS (1) ACTIVE & RESPONSIBLE

DATE _____

LEARNING GOALS

At the conclusion of this activity, I will be able to;

- Explain the first two Wellbeing Indicators - Active and Responsible
- Identify ways in which the Wellbeing Indicators are already present in my life
- Reflect on how skilled and confident I am at physical activities and at making healthy choices

JOURNAL ACTIVITY: (A) WELLBEING INDICATOR - ACTIVE

1. List 3 ways you are physically active.

    → _____
    → _____
    → _____

2. Using the scale below, with 1 being very low and 10 being very high, how confident are you at these activities?

1	2	3	4	5	6	7	8	9	10

JOURNAL ACTIVITY: (B) WELLBEING INDICATOR - RESPONSIBLE

1. List 3 ways in which you protect and promote your wellbeing and that of others.

    → _____
    → _____
    → _____

2. List 3 healthy eating choices you make.

    → _____
    → _____
    → _____

3. List 3 areas where your safety is at risk.

    → _____
    → _____
    → _____

4. List 3 choices you make to keep yourself and others safe.

→ _____

→ _____

→ _____

JOURNAL ACTIVITY: (C) HOMEWORK

Write one way in which you will change to:

a) Develop your level of activity:	b) Be more responsible:

LESSON REVIEW

3-2-1

3 THINGS I LEARNED TODAY _____

_____

_____

2 THINGS I WILL CHANGE/IMPROVE _____

_____

1 THING I WANT TO KNOW MORE ABOUT _____

TRAFFIC LIGHTS

COLOUR THE TRAFFIC LIGHT WHICH BEST REPRESENTS YOUR UNDERSTANDING IN TODAY'S LESSON

Red: I don't understand at all and need help

Orange: I need some support and don't fully understand some aspects of what we learned about

Green: I am happy that I understand this lesson very well

INDICATORS OF WELLBEING

TICK THE BOX TO SHOW THE INDICATORS OF WELLBEING YOU IDENTIFY IN TODAY'S LESSON

LEARNING GOALS

At the conclusion of this activity, I will be able to;

- Explain the third and fourth Wellbeing Indicators - Connected and Resilient
- Identify ways in which the Wellbeing Indicators are already present in my life
- Reflect on how connected I am to the people and the world around me and how resilient I am in facing life's challenges

JOURNAL ACTIVITY: (A) WELLBEING INDICATOR - CONNECTED

1. What does the term 'Connected' mean?

_____

2. List one way you are already connected to each of the following:

(a) School: _____ _____	(b) Friends: _____ _____
(c) Local Community: _____ _____	(d) Wider World: _____ _____

3. How do your actions and interactions impact on your own wellbeing and that of others in:

(a) Local Context: _____ _____	(b) Global Context: _____ _____

JOURNAL ACTIVITY: (B) WELLBEING INDICATOR - RESILIENT

1. What does the term 'Resilient' mean?

_____

2. List 2 ways in which you have already coped with life's challenges.

→ _____

→ _____

3. Do you know where to go for help? Give 2 examples (Refer to Lesson 2).

→ _____

→ _____

4. Describe 2 examples of when you achieved something due to the effort you put in.

→ _____

→ _____

JOURNAL ACTIVITY: (C) HOMEWORK

Write one way in which you will change in order to:

a) Develop your level of connectedness:	b) Be more resilient:

LESSON REVIEW

3-2-1

3 THINGS I LEARNED TODAY _____

_____

_____

2 THINGS I WILL CHANGE/IMPROVE _____

_____

1 THING I WANT TO KNOW MORE ABOUT _____

TRAFFIC LIGHTS

COLOUR THE TRAFFIC LIGHT WHICH BEST REPRESENTS YOUR UNDERSTANDING IN TODAY'S LESSON

Red: I don't understand at all and need help

Orange: I need some support and don't fully understand some aspects of what we learned about

Green: I am happy that I understand this lesson very well

INDICATORS OF WELLBEING

TICK THE BOX TO SHOW THE INDICATORS OF WELLBEING YOU IDENTIFY IN TODAY'S LESSON

LESSON 5 - WELLBEING INDICATORS (3) RESPECTED & AWARE

LEARNING GOALS

At the conclusion of this activity, I will be able to;

- Explain the fifth and sixth Wellbeing Indicators - Respected and Aware
- Identify ways the Wellbeing Indicators are already present in my life
- Reflect on how respected I feel, how aware I am of my emotions and thought processes and my capacity to learn and improve

JOURNAL ACTIVITY: (A) WELLBEING INDICATOR - RESPECTED

1. List one way in which you feel you are respected and valued by others.

_____

2. Give an example of a positive respectful relationship you have with each of the following:

(a) A Friend:	(b) A Family Member:	(c) A Teacher:
_____ _____	_____ _____	_____ _____

3. Why do you think it is important for people to respect each other, each other's property / belongings and each other's feelings?

_____

_____

JOURNAL ACTIVITY: (B) WELLBEING INDICATOR - AWARE

1. When and where do you do your best thinking?

_____

_____

2. Give an example of a behaviour you display when you feel each of the following:

A Positive Emotion:
A Negative Emotion:

3. When you are aware of negative emotions, what can you do to improve your mood?

_____

JOURNAL ACTIVITY: (C) HOMEWORK

Describe 2 things you do which help you to learn.

1. _____

2. _____

Write 2 things you could do to improve the way in which you learn.

1. _____

2. _____

LESSON REVIEW

3-2-1

3 THINGS I LEARNED TODAY

_____

_____

_____

2 THINGS I WILL CHANGE/IMPROVE

_____

_____

1 THING I WANT TO KNOW MORE ABOUT

_____

TRAFFIC LIGHTS

COLOUR THE TRAFFIC LIGHT WHICH BEST REPRESENTS YOUR UNDERSTANDING IN TODAY'S LESSON

Red: I don't understand at all and need help

Orange: I need some support and don't fully understand some aspects of what we learned about

Green: I am happy that I understand this lesson very well

INDICATORS OF WELLBEING

TICK THE BOX TO SHOW THE INDICATORS OF WELLBEING YOU IDENTIFY IN TODAY'S LESSON

LEARNING GOALS

At the conclusion of this activity, I will be able to;

- Identify new information about my classmates
- Compile a bank of facts about my peers in an activity of Classroom Bingo
- Reflect upon my learning using a reflective exercise in my Student Journal

JOURNAL ACTIVITY: (A) BINGO!

1. You must try to find classmates who meet the descriptions in the boxes below.
2. When you find somebody who fits the description in the box, ask them to sign their name in the relevant box.
3. Shout "BINGO!" once you have completed the entire Bingo grid.
4. Once someone shouts "BINGO!" return to your seat. This person may introduce those who signed their sheet.

B	I	N	G	O
Was born abroad	Plays on a school sports team	Has brown/black hair	Has been involved in voluntary work	Can swim
Likes to read	Is doing art in school	Went to a different primary school	Has 2 siblings	Has a birthday this month
Can whistle	Has been to France	Likes to play basketball	Plays a musical instrument	Has a pet

JOURNAL ACTIVITY: (B) REFLECTION

1. Did you know any of the students in your class before you started 1st Year?

2. Did anything you learned today surprise you?

3. Did you enjoy this activity? Explain your answer.

LESSON REVIEW

3-2-1

3 THINGS I LEARNED TODAY

2 THINGS I WILL CHANGE/IMPROVE

1 THING I WANT TO KNOW MORE ABOUT

TRAFFIC LIGHTS

COLOUR THE TRAFFIC LIGHT WHICH BEST REPRESENTS YOUR UNDERSTANDING IN TODAY'S LESSON

Red: I don't understand at all and need help

Orange: I need some support and don't fully understand some aspects of what we learned about

Green: I am happy that I understand this lesson very well

INDICATORS OF WELLBEING

TICK THE BOX TO SHOW THE INDICATORS OF WELLBEING YOU IDENTIFY IN TODAY'S LESSON

LEARNING GOALS

At the conclusion of this activity, I will be able to;

- Identify the changes I have experienced during the transition from primary to secondary school
- Give examples of my ideas to a partner and share them with the class
- Outline an individual goal to reach in the next few months of 1st Year

JOURNAL ACTIVITY: (A) THINK, PAIR, SHARE

Think about the questions below.

1. **Think:** Work alone and write your answer in the 1st box.
2. **Pair:** Work with your partner, discuss your ideas and write them in the 2nd box.
3. **Share:** Share your ideas with the class and write some new ideas in the 3rd box.

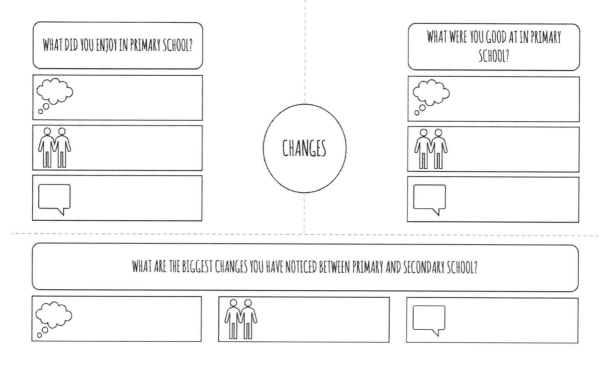

JOURNAL ACTIVITY: (B) REFLECTION

You have already explored some of the changes you are just beginning to experience as you begin life after primary school. Take time to reflect upon the following questions and write down how you feel about them.

1. What excites you / what are you looking forward to?
2. What are your fears or concerns?
3. What do you hope to have accomplished by Christmas? (e.g. made a new friend / learned all my teachers' names / understood my timetable fully).

REFLECTION

LESSON REVIEW

3-2-1

3 THINGS I LEARNED TODAY _____

_____

_____

2 THINGS I WILL CHANGE/IMPROVE _____

_____

1 THING I WANT TO KNOW MORE ABOUT _____

TRAFFIC LIGHTS

COLOUR THE TRAFFIC LIGHT WHICH BEST REPRESENTS YOUR UNDERSTANDING IN TODAY'S LESSON

Red: I don't understand at all and need help

Orange: I need some support and don't fully understand some aspects of what we learned about

Green: I am happy that I understand this lesson very well

INDICATORS OF WELLBEING

TICK THE BOX TO SHOW THE INDICATORS OF WELLBEING YOU IDENTIFY IN TODAY'S LESSON

LEARNING GOALS

At the conclusion of this activity, I will be able to;

- Identify my own current level of organisation
- Recognise the impact of being organised at school
- Produce a plan to implement three new strategies to improve my organisational skills

JOURNAL ACTIVITY: (A) SELF ASSESSMENT

Answer 'yes' or 'no' the following questions. Be as honest as you can.

1. Do you wear a watch? _____

2. Have you ever lost your phone? _____

3. Do you set your own alarm for the morning the night before? _____

4. Would you describe your bedroom as clean and tidy? _____

5. Do you record all of your homework in your journal? _____

6. Is your homework space quiet and organised? _____

7. Do you write lists and stick to them? _____

JOURNAL ACTIVITY: (B) NEW HINTS & TIPS

MY TOP 3 ORGANISATION HINTS & TIPS TO TRY THIS WEEK

1. _____

2. _____

3. _____

LESSON REVIEW

3-2-1

3 THINGS I LEARNED TODAY

2 THINGS I WILL CHANGE/IMPROVE

1 THING I WANT TO KNOW MORE ABOUT

TRAFFIC LIGHTS

COLOUR THE TRAFFIC LIGHT WHICH BEST REPRESENTS YOUR UNDERSTANDING IN TODAY'S LESSON

Red: I don't understand at all and need help

Orange: I need some support and don't fully understand some aspects of what we learned about

Green: I am happy that I understand this lesson very well

INDICATORS OF WELLBEING

TICK THE BOX TO SHOW THE INDICATORS OF WELLBEING YOU IDENTIFY IN TODAY'S LESSON

LESSON 9 - BEING ORGANISED (2) MY WEEK

DATE _ _ _ _ _ _ _ _ _

LEARNING GOALS

At the conclusion of this activity, I will be able to;

- Reflect upon what did or didn't work this week in relation to my organisational skills
- Identify ways to make further improvements to my level of organisation on a daily basis
- Develop a plan for my week, including all of my activities and commitments

JOURNAL ACTIVITY: (A) RAPID RECAP

In the previous lesson you recorded 3 things you would try to do during the week in order to improve your organisational skills at school. Now, take time to reflect upon the following:

1. What 3 hints and tips you used this week.

_____

_____

2. What worked or didn't work for you.

_____

_____

3. What you will try in the week ahead to keep improving your level of organisation in school.

_____

_____

PERSONAL REFLECTION

JOURNAL ACTIVITY: (B) MY WEEKLY TIMETABLE

TIME	MONDAY	TUESDAY	WEDNESDAY	THURSDAY	FRIDAY
MY WEEK					
	School	School	School	School	School
	Bed time	Bed time	Bed time	Bed time	Bed time

LESSON REVIEW

3-2-1

3 THINGS I LEARNED TODAY

_____

_____

_____

2 THINGS I WILL CHANGE/IMPROVE

_____

_____

1 THING I WANT TO KNOW MORE ABOUT

_____

TRAFFIC LIGHTS

COLOUR THE TRAFFIC LIGHT WHICH BEST REPRESENTS YOUR UNDERSTANDING IN TODAY'S LESSON

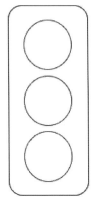

Red: I don't understand at all and need help

Orange: I need some support and don't fully understand some aspects of what we learned about

Green: I am happy that I understand this lesson very well

INDICATORS OF WELLBEING

TICK THE BOX TO SHOW THE INDICATORS OF WELLBEING YOU IDENTIFY IN TODAY'S LESSON

LEARNING GOALS

At the conclusion of this activity, I will be able to;

- Discuss and give examples of good organisational skills
- Analyse my own personal organisational habits
- Identify and list ways in which I can improve my own personal organisational habits

JOURNAL ACTIVITY: (A) ORGANISATIONAL SCALE

Using the scale below, with 1 being very low and 10 being very high, colour in the boxes to answer the questions.

1.   How organised is your school journal?

1	2	3	4	5	6	7	8	9	10

2. How organised is your school bag?

1	2	3	4	5	6	7	8	9	10

3. How organised is your school locker?

1	2	3	4	5	6	7	8	9	10

4. How organised is your homework and study space at home?

1	2	3	4	5	6	7	8	9	10

JOURNAL ACTIVITY: (B) MAKE A LIST

List 7 new ways in which you will improve your own personal organisational skills.

1. _____

2. _____

3. _____

4. _____

5. _____

6. _____

7. _____

LESSON REVIEW

3-2-1

3 THINGS I LEARNED TODAY

_____

_____

_____

2 THINGS I WILL CHANGE/IMPROVE

_____

_____

1 THING I WANT TO KNOW MORE ABOUT

_____

TRAFFIC LIGHTS

COLOUR THE TRAFFIC LIGHT WHICH BEST REPRESENTS YOUR UNDERSTANDING IN TODAY'S LESSON

Red: I don't understand at all and need help

Orange: I need some support and don't fully understand some aspects of what we learned about

Green: I am happy that I understand this lesson very well

INDICATORS OF WELLBEING

TICK THE BOX TO SHOW THE INDICATORS OF WELLBEING YOU IDENTIFY IN TODAY'S LESSON

LEARNING GOALS

At the conclusion of this activity, I will be able to;

- Give examples of the Wellbeing Indicators in everyday life
- Interpret a news article and identify Wellbeing Indicators within it
- Plan a poster which outlines one Wellbeing Indicator being shown in my school, local or wider community

JOURNAL ACTIVITY: (A) INDICATOR WHEEL

Using the Indicator Wheel below, write one example of each of the 6 Wellbeing Indicators showing people in your community who display that particular characteristic.

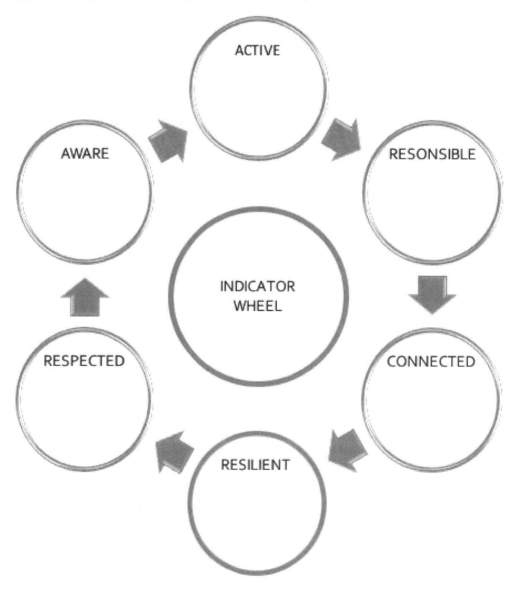

JOURNAL ACTIVITY: (B) POSTER PLANNING

Choose partner →	
Choose article →	
Share tasks fairly →	

LESSON REVIEW

3-2-1

3 THINGS I LEARNED TODAY   _____

_____

_____

2 THINGS I WILL CHANGE/IMPROVE   _____

_____

1 THING I WANT TO KNOW MORE ABOUT   _____

TRAFFIC LIGHTS

COLOUR THE TRAFFIC LIGHT WHICH BEST REPRESENTS YOUR
UNDERSTANDING IN TODAY'S LESSON

Red: I don't understand at all and need help

Orange: I need some support and don't fully understand some aspects of what we learned about

Green: I am happy that I understand this lesson very well

INDICATORS OF WELLBEING

TICK THE BOX TO SHOW THE INDICATORS OF WELLBEING YOU
IDENTIFY IN TODAY'S LESSON

LESSON 12 – INDICATORS IN ACTION (2) POSTER & PRESENTATIONS

DATE _ _ _ _ _ _ _ _ _

LEARNING GOALS

At the conclusion of this activity, I will be able to;

- Present my 'Indicators in Action' poster to my peers in an Oral Presentation
- Critique three of my peers' presentations (based on headings given)
- Give feedback to my peer in verbal and written format

JOURNAL ACTIVITY: (A) PRESENTATION FEEDBACK

Poster 1. Group name: _____

★ Write **one positive comment** about the presentation.

_____
_____
_____

★ Write **one question** you would like to ask about the presentation.

_____
_____

★ Write **one suggestion** you think would help improve the presentation.

_____
_____

Poster 2. Group name: _____

★ Write **one positive comment** about the presentation.

_____
_____
_____

★ Write **one question** you would like to ask about the presentation.

_____
_____

★ Write **one suggestion** you think would help improve the presentation.

_____
_____

Poster 3. Group name: _____

★ Write **one positive comment** about the presentation.

_____
_____
_____

★ Write **one question** you would like to ask about the presentation.

_____
_____

★ Write **one suggestion** you think would help improve the presentation.

_____
_____

LESSON REVIEW

3-2-1

3 THINGS I LEARNED TODAY

_____

_____

_____

2 THINGS I WILL CHANGE/IMPROVE

_____

_____

1 THING I WANT TO KNOW MORE ABOUT

_____

TRAFFIC LIGHTS

COLOUR THE TRAFFIC LIGHT WHICH BEST REPRESENTS YOUR UNDERSTANDING IN TODAY'S LESSON

Red: I don't understand at all and need help

Orange: I need some support and don't fully understand some aspects of what we learned about

Green: I am happy that I understand this lesson very well

INDICATORS OF WELLBEING

TICK THE BOX TO SHOW THE INDICATORS OF WELLBEING YOU IDENTIFY IN TODAY'S LESSON

LESSON 13 - POSITIVE AFFIRMATIONS (1)　　　　　　　　DATE _____

LEARNING GOALS

At the conclusion of this activity, I will be able to;

- Examine the meaning of the term 'Positive Affirmation'
- Give examples of 'Positive Affirmations'
- Create a sentence containing 'Positive Affirmations' about myself using as many letters of the alphabet as possible

JOURNAL ACTIVITY: (A) WORDS THAT START WITH… A, B, C…

Complete the sentence to create a positive affirmation using the letters below. For example, I am … **a**ctive. I am …**b**rave. etc.

'I am…'

A _____　　　B _____

C _____　　　D _____

E _____　　　F _____

G _____　　　H _____

I _____　　　J _____

K _____　　　L _____

M _____　　　N _____

O _____　　　P _____

Q _____　　　R _____

S _____   T _____

U _____   V _____

W _____   X _____

Y _____   Z _____

LESSON REVIEW

3-2-1

3 THINGS I LEARNED TODAY   _____

                                _____

                                _____

2 THINGS I WILL CHANGE/IMPROVE _____

                                _____

1 THING I WANT TO KNOW MORE ABOUT _____

TRAFFIC LIGHTS

COLOUR THE TRAFFIC LIGHT WHICH BEST REPRESENTS YOUR
UNDERSTANDING IN TODAY'S LESSON

Red: I don't understand at all and need help

Orange: I need some support and don't fully understand some aspects of what we learned about

Green: I am happy that I understand this lesson very well

INDICATORS OF WELLBEING

TICK THE BOX TO SHOW THE INDICATORS OF WELLBEING YOU
IDENTIFY IN TODAY'S LESSON

LEARNING GOALS

At the conclusion of this activity, I will be able to;

- Examine the meaning of the term 'Positive Affirmation'
- Give examples of 'Positive Affirmations'
- Design and create a bookmark for myself containing a 'Positive Affirmation'

JOURNAL ACTIVITY: (A) REFLECTION

Having designed and created a bookmark for yourself containing a 'Positive Affirmation', write about your thoughts and feelings about the creative process, e.g. Did you enjoy creating the bookmark? Did you find it relaxing? What was the biggest challenge for you?

_____

_____

_____

_____

_____

_____

_____

_____

_____

_____

_____

_____

_____

_____

_____

_____

_____

_____

_____

_____

_____

_____

_____

_____

_____

_____

_____

_____

_____

LESSON REVIEW

3-2-1

3 THINGS I LEARNED TODAY _____

_____

_____

2 THINGS I WILL CHANGE/IMPROVE _____

_____

1 THING I WANT TO KNOW MORE ABOUT _____

TRAFFIC LIGHTS

COLOUR THE TRAFFIC LIGHT WHICH BEST REPRESENTS YOUR
UNDERSTANDING IN TODAY'S LESSON

Red: I don't understand at all and need help

Orange: I need some support and don't fully understand some aspects of what we learned about

Green: I am happy that I understand this lesson very well

INDICATORS OF WELLBEING

TICK THE BOX TO SHOW THE INDICATORS OF WELLBEING YOU
IDENTIFY IN TODAY'S LESSON

LESSON 15 - BEING ORGANISED (4) RECAP

DATE _____

LEARNING GOALS

At the conclusion of this activity, I will be able to;

- Reflect upon the importance of a clear mind and the ability to focus
- Discuss with a partner strategies you have implemented to become more organised
- Identify a new way to improve your planning and organisational skills

JOURNAL ACTIVITY: (A) BRAIN DUMP

As you listen to the music, jot down any thoughts that come into your mind.

JOURNAL ACTIVITY: (B) INTERVIEWS

Interview your partner and answer the following:

1. What did your partner do over the past few weeks to help become more organised?

_____

_____

2. What strategies worked most effectively for you both?

_____

_____

3. What strategy are each of you going to work on next?

_____

_____

LESSON REVIEW

3-2-1

3 THINGS I LEARNED TODAY

_____

_____

_____

2 THINGS I WILL CHANGE/IMPROVE

_____

_____

1 THING I WANT TO KNOW MORE ABOUT

_____

TRAFFIC LIGHTS

COLOUR THE TRAFFIC LIGHT WHICH BEST REPRESENTS YOUR UNDERSTANDING IN TODAY'S LESSON

Red: I don't understand at all and need help

Orange: I need some support and don't fully understand some aspects of what we learned about

Green: I am happy that I understand this lesson very well

INDICATORS OF WELLBEING

TICK THE BOX TO SHOW THE INDICATORS OF WELLBEING YOU IDENTIFY IN TODAY'S LESSON

LESSON 16 - REFLECTION TIME (2) 1ST YEAR IN SECONDARY SCHOOL SO FAR

DATE _____

LEARNING GOALS

At the conclusion of this activity, I will be able to;

- Identify the challenges I have experienced and overcome to date during the transition from primary to secondary school
- Give examples of other challenges which I face in 1st year
- Outline positive ways in which I can overcome these challenges

JOURNAL ACTIVITY: (A) DIAMOND 9

List 9 challenges which you have overcome in 1st year in secondary school so far.

1. _____
2. _____
3. _____
4. _____
5. _____
6. _____
7. _____
8. _____
9. _____

Now, using the 'Diamond 9' worksheet provided, prioritise these challenges. The most important challenge is placed towards the top of the 'diamond' and the least important challenge towards the bottom. Challenges of equal importance are placed on the same row.

JOURNAL ACTIVITY: (B) REFLECTION

WELL DONE! You have explored, prioritised and shared challenges you have already overcome since starting 1st year in secondary school.

Take time to reflect upon the following and write down how you feel about them.

1. What one challenge are you currently experiencing in 1st year and finding difficult to overcome? (e.g. specific subject, subject topic, managing homework, completing project work, etc.).
2. Think about how you can overcome this challenge. Write down positive steps to overcome this challenge.
3. Who can you ask for help to overcome this challenge?

PERSONAL REFLECTION

LESSON REVIEW

3-2-1

3 THINGS I LEARNED TODAY

_____

_____

_____

2 THINGS I WILL CHANGE/IMPROVE

_____

_____

1 THING I WANT TO KNOW MORE ABOUT

_____

TRAFFIC LIGHTS

COLOUR THE TRAFFIC LIGHT WHICH BEST REPRESENTS YOUR UNDERSTANDING IN TODAY'S LESSON

Red: I don't understand at all and need help

Orange: I need some support and don't fully understand some aspects of what we learned about

Green: I am happy that I understand this lesson very well

INDICATORS OF WELLBEING

TICK THE BOX TO SHOW THE INDICATORS OF WELLBEING YOU IDENTIFY IN TODAY'S LESSON

LESSON 17 - STRENGTHS AND WEAKNESSES   DATE _ _ _ _ _ _ _ _

LEARNING GOALS

At the conclusion of this activity, I will be able to;

- Identify my strengths and weaknesses
- Explore how my current interests reveal my strengths and reflect on areas for improvement
- Set goals, noting the steps I will need to take in order to achieve these

JOURNAL ACTIVITY: (A) THINK, PAIR, SHARE

MY STRENGTHS **Think** about your current interests, talents, skills...	MY WEAKNESSES **Think** about things you struggle with / find difficult...

Pair: Discuss your answers with your partner.

Share: Put your group's main points on the 'Strengths and Weaknesses' sheet provided.

JOURNAL ACTIVITY: (B) REFLECTION

1. What areas of weakness would you like to improve on this term?

_____

_____

2. What would you like to achieve this term?

_____

_____

3. What steps must you take in order to achieve this?

_____

_____

_____

_____

4. What other supports might you need to be successful in achieving this?

_____

_____

_____

_____

LESSON REVIEW

3-2-1

3 THINGS I LEARNED TODAY
_____

_____

_____

2 THINGS I WILL CHANGE/IMPROVE
_____

_____

1 THING I WANT TO KNOW MORE ABOUT
_____

TRAFFIC LIGHTS

COLOUR THE TRAFFIC LIGHT WHICH BEST REPRESENTS YOUR UNDERSTANDING IN TODAY'S LESSON

Red: I don't understand at all and need help

Orange: I need some support and don't fully understand some aspects of what we learned about

Green: I am happy that I understand this lesson very well

INDICATORS OF WELLBEING

TICK THE BOX TO SHOW THE INDICATORS OF WELLBEING YOU IDENTIFY IN TODAY'S LESSON

LEARNING GOALS

At the conclusion of this activity, I will be able to;

- Define the meaning of a 'goal'
- Outline my own goals for this year
- Plan the steps that I need to take in order to achieve 2 of my goals

JOURNAL ACTIVITY: (A) THINK, PAIR, SHARE

What are some of the goals that you would like to achieve this year?

i. _____

ii. _____

iii. _____

iv. _____

v. _____

vi. _____

vii. _____

JOURNAL ACTIVITY: (B) SETTING MY GOALS

Now, narrow it down and choose 2 main goals you wish to focus on.

My 1st main goal is...	
I want to achieve this by...	
Possible challenges/obstacles are...	
Steps I need to take to achieve my goal...	

My 2ⁿᵈ main goal is...	
I want to achieve this by...	
Possible challenges/obstacles are...	
Steps I need to take to achieve my goal...	

LESSON REVIEW

3-2-1

3 THINGS I LEARNED TODAY _____

_____

_____

2 THINGS I WILL CHANGE/IMPROVE _____

_____

1 THING I WANT TO KNOW MORE ABOUT _____

TRAFFIC LIGHTS

COLOUR THE TRAFFIC LIGHT WHICH BEST REPRESENTS YOUR UNDERSTANDING IN TODAY'S LESSON

Red: I don't understand at all and need help

Orange: I need some support and don't fully understand some aspects of what we learned about

Green: I am happy that I understand this lesson very well

INDICATORS OF WELLBEING

TICK THE BOX TO SHOW THE INDICATORS OF WELLBEING YOU IDENTIFY IN TODAY'S LESSON

LESSON 19 - ANTI-BULLYING (1) UNDERSTANDING BULLYING

DATE _____

LEARNING GOALS

At the conclusion of this activity, I will be able to;

- Express my thoughts about bullying
- Discuss ways I think the school should respond to bullying issues
- Record / present my ideas and compare them with those of others

JOURNAL ACTIVITY: (A) QUESTIONS

Discuss the following questions with your group / partner and write your answers below. You will then be asked to report your answers to your classmates.

1. How can the school enable students to report bullying?

_____

_____

2. What should a teacher do if someone reports bullying?

_____

_____

_____

3. How should the person accused of bullying be dealt with?

_____

_____

_____

4. How should the person being bullied be treated?

_____

_____

_____

5. What can the school do to prevent bullying?

_____

_____

_____

JOURNAL ACTIVITY: (B) REPORTER FEEDBACK

Write any new information which you have received during the reporter feedback task.

LESSON REVIEW

3-2-1

3 THINGS I LEARNED TODAY   _____

_____

_____

2 THINGS I WILL CHANGE/IMPROVE   _____

_____

1 THING I WANT TO KNOW MORE ABOUT   _____

TRAFFIC LIGHTS

COLOUR THE TRAFFIC LIGHT WHICH BEST REPRESENTS YOUR
UNDERSTANDING IN TODAY'S LESSON

Red: I don't understand at all and
need help

Orange: I need some support and
don't fully understand some aspects
of what we learned about

Green: I am happy that I understand
this lesson very well

INDICATORS OF WELLBEING

TICK THE BOX TO SHOW THE INDICATORS OF WELLBEING YOU
IDENTIFY IN TODAY'S LESSON

LESSON 20 - ANTI-BULLYING (2) OUR SCHOOL'S POLICY

LEARNING GOALS

At the conclusion of this activity, I will be able to;

- Reflect on my thoughts about the school's Anti-Bullying Policy
- Select the key words / phrases from the policy which resonate with me
- Record the key steps I need to take if I witness bullying or if I am being bullied

JOURNAL ACTIVITY: (A) ACTIVE LISTENING

1. In the boxes below: Make a note of the key words / phrases from the Anti-Bullying Policy. You will use these in the next lesson.

2. What are the steps you need to take if you see bullying happening or you are being bullied yourself?

→ _____

→ _____

→ _____

→ _____

→ _____

→ _____

3. What do you do if the bullying happens again and/or persists?

_____

_____

_____

_____

JOURNAL ACTIVITY: (B) REFLECTION

Pick 3 positive things you like about the school's Anti-Bullying Policy and explain why you liked them.

1. _____
   _____

2. _____
   _____

3. _____
   _____

LESSON REVIEW

3-2-1

3 THINGS I LEARNED TODAY   _____

_____

_____

2 THINGS I WILL CHANGE/IMPROVE   _____

_____

1 THING I WANT TO KNOW MORE ABOUT   _____

TRAFFIC LIGHTS

COLOUR THE TRAFFIC LIGHT WHICH BEST REPRESENTS YOUR UNDERSTANDING IN TODAY'S LESSON

Red: I don't understand at all and need help

Orange: I need some support and don't fully understand some aspects of what we learned about

Green: I am happy that I understand this lesson very well

INDICATORS OF WELLBEING

TICK THE BOX TO SHOW THE INDICATORS OF WELLBEING YOU IDENTIFY IN TODAY'S LESSON

LESSON 21 - ANTI-BULLYING (3) POSTER COMPETITION

LEARNING GOALS

At the conclusion of this activity, I will be able to;

- Use selected key words from the school's Anti-Bullying Policy in poster format
- Design an anti-bullying poster
- Execute my design, creating a finished product

JOURNAL ACTIVITY: (A) PLAN YOUR POSTER DESIGN

1. Look back at Lesson 20 and write some **key words / phrases** from the school's Anti-Bullying Policy below that you would like to use in your poster design.

2. What message do you want to get across in your poster design?

_____

_____

_____

3. How do you plan on getting this message across?

_____

_____

_____

_____

4. What other important information do you want to convey?

_____

_____

_____

_____

_____

5. How will you reflect that in a visual image?

_____

_____

_____

_____

_____

_____

_____

_____

LESSON REVIEW

3-2-1

3 THINGS I LEARNED TODAY

_____

_____

_____

2 THINGS I WILL CHANGE/IMPROVE

_____

_____

1 THING I WANT TO KNOW MORE ABOUT

_____

TRAFFIC LIGHTS

COLOUR THE TRAFFIC LIGHT WHICH BEST REPRESENTS YOUR UNDERSTANDING IN TODAY'S LESSON

Red: I don't understand at all and need help

Orange: I need some support and don't fully understand some aspects of what we learned about

Green: I am happy that I understand this lesson very well

INDICATORS OF WELLBEING

TICK THE BOX TO SHOW THE INDICATORS OF WELLBEING YOU IDENTIFY IN TODAY'S LESSON

LEARNING GOALS

At the conclusion of this activity, I will be able to;

- Recognise my feelings in relation to older students in the school
- Explore ideas and possibilities in order to organise an activity with older students in the school
- Share roles with classmates and take responsibility for various tasks

JOURNAL ACTIVITY: (A) BRAINDROPS

Use the raindrops to write down all the ideas you can think of for a fun lesson with older students in the school.

JOURNAL ACTIVITY: (B) PLANNING

Event planning & My Responsibilities			
Area in the school being used			
Day & time of event			
My tasks	To do	With	Due date
1			
2			
3			

LESSON REVIEW

3-2-1

3 THINGS I LEARNED TODAY

_____

_____

_____

2 THINGS I WILL CHANGE/IMPROVE

_____

_____

1 THING I WANT TO KNOW MORE ABOUT

_____

TRAFFIC LIGHTS

COLOUR THE TRAFFIC LIGHT WHICH BEST REPRESENTS YOUR UNDERSTANDING IN TODAY'S LESSON

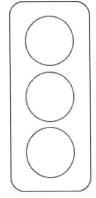

Red: I don't understand at all and need help

Orange: I need some support and don't fully understand some aspects of what we learned about

Green: I am happy that I understand this lesson very well

INDICATORS OF WELLBEING

TICK THE BOX TO SHOW THE INDICATORS OF WELLBEING YOU IDENTIFY IN TODAY'S LESSON

49

LESSON 23 – 1ST YEAR & 6TH YEAR SOCIAL EVENT (2) EXECUTION

DATE _ _ _ _ _ _ _ _

LEARNING GOALS

At the conclusion of this activity, I will be able to;

- Complete the assigned individual tasks effectively
- Execute a class project based on planning in previous lesson
- Reflect upon my experience of interacting with 6th year students and learning in the lesson

JOURNAL ACTIVITY: (A) REFLECTION

1. What event did you and your peers plan for the senior students?

_____

_____

2. Describe what you were responsible for in preparing for this event.

_____

_____

_____

_____

_____

3. Did you enjoy planning and running this event? Why?

_____

_____

_____

_____

_____

4. Who did you meet and what did you learn from them?

_____

_____

_____

_____

_____

5. What did you learn about planning events with your peers?

_____

_____

_____

_____

6. What did you learn about yourself?

_____

_____

_____

_____

_____

7. What would you do differently if you were to plan an activity like this in future?

_____

_____

_____

_____

_____

LESSON REVIEW

3-2-1

3 THINGS I LEARNED TODAY

_____

_____

_____

2 THINGS I WILL CHANGE/IMPROVE

_____

_____

1 THING I WANT TO KNOW MORE ABOUT

_____

TRAFFIC LIGHTS

COLOUR THE TRAFFIC LIGHT WHICH BEST REPRESENTS YOUR UNDERSTANDING IN TODAY'S LESSON

Red: I don't understand at all and need help

Orange: I need some support and don't fully understand some aspects of what we learned about

Green: I am happy that I understand this lesson very well

INDICATORS OF WELLBEING

TICK THE BOX TO SHOW THE INDICATORS OF WELLBEING YOU IDENTIFY IN TODAY'S LESSON

LEARNING GOALS

At the conclusion of this activity, I will be able to;

- Recognise and respect differences between myself and my classmates
- Identify ways in which I feel I learn best
- Define the type of learner I am and characteristics of this learning style

JOURNAL ACTIVITY: (A) QUIZ TIME!

For each question, select the most appropriate answer for you!

When I study for a test, I...	When I listen to music, I...
a. Write and draw b. Read notes c. Have someone ask me questions	a. Tap my foot b. Daydream c. Hum and sing along
If given the choice, I would prefer to go to... a. PE class b. Art class c. Music class	**I learn best in class when my teacher...** a. Teaches us a song with actions b. Shows pictures on a PowerPoint c. Teaches us a rhyme or poem
I remember information best from... a. Doing a science experiment b. Watching a video c. Hearing a podcast	**My favourite questions in a test...** a. Asks me to use a tool (e.g. ruler) b. Includes graphs or charts c. Are read out loud
My favourite type of book... a. Has puzzles and activities in it b. Has lots of pictures in it c. Has lots of words in it	**To find a new place, you...** a. Walk around until you find it b. Use a map to direct you c. Ask someone for directions

How many of each did you get?		
A=	B=	C=

What is your strongest learning style(s)?

Mostly A's =   I'm a kinaesthetic learner

Mostly B's =   I'm a visual learner

Mostly C's =   I'm an auditory learner

JOURNAL ACTIVITY: (B) LEARNING STYLES

Record what you are learning about each learning style. Pay close attention to your strongest style(s)!		
Kinaesthetic	Visual	Auditory

LESSON REVIEW

3-2-1

3 THINGS I LEARNED TODAY

_____

_____

_____

2 THINGS I WILL CHANGE/IMPROVE

_____

_____

1 THING I WANT TO KNOW MORE ABOUT

_____

TRAFFIC LIGHTS

COLOUR THE TRAFFIC LIGHT WHICH BEST REPRESENTS YOUR UNDERSTANDING IN TODAY'S LESSON

Red: I don't understand at all and need help

Orange: I need some support and don't fully understand some aspects of what we learned about

Green: I am happy that I understand this lesson very well

INDICATORS OF WELLBEING

TICK THE BOX TO SHOW THE INDICATORS OF WELLBEING YOU IDENTIFY IN TODAY'S LESSON

LESSON 25 - HOW TO STUDY SMART (1)   DATE _____

LEARNING GOALS

At the conclusion of this activity, I will be able to;

- Identify learning strategies for kinaesthetic, visual and auditory learners
- Select strategies which will suit me best in my learning
- Apply a learning strategy to my school work

JOURNAL ACTIVITY: (A) LEARNING STRATEGIES

Record what strategies you are learning about for each learning style.

Highlight the most useful study techniques for you based on your learning style Record as many as you can!		
Kinaesthetic	Visual	Auditory

JOURNAL ACTIVITY: (B) TRY IT OUT!

Use the space below to try out one of the learning strategies you have identified.

LESSON REVIEW

3-2-1

3 THINGS I LEARNED TODAY

_____

_____

_____

2 THINGS I WILL CHANGE/IMPROVE

_____

_____

1 THING I WANT TO KNOW MORE ABOUT

_____

TRAFFIC LIGHTS

COLOUR THE TRAFFIC LIGHT WHICH BEST REPRESENTS YOUR UNDERSTANDING IN TODAY'S LESSON

Red: I don't understand at all and need help

Orange: I need some support and don't fully understand some aspects of what we learned about

Green: I am happy that I understand this lesson very well

INDICATORS OF WELLBEING

TICK THE BOX TO SHOW THE INDICATORS OF WELLBEING YOU IDENTIFY IN TODAY'S LESSON

LESSON 26 - HOW TO STUDY SMART (2)

DATE _____

LEARNING GOALS

At the conclusion of this activity, I will be able to;

- Work with a partner to give examples of how to study effectively
- Give examples of study hints and tips, using the acronym SMART TIPS
- Apply SMART TIPS to my study and revision planning

JOURNAL ACTIVITY: (A) BLUE SKY

- ✓ Blue Sky is an opportunity for you to use your imagination!
- ✓ Work with a partner and write all of your ideas for study hints and tips below.
- ✓ Don't be afraid to suggest or write down an idea. Even if it isn't used in the end, it may help someone else think outside the box too!

IDEAS: STUDY HINTS & TIPS

Examples:
- *Organise books and copies in advance*
- *Set a time every day to revise*

JOURNAL ACTIVITY: (B) SMART TIPS

List what each letter of the acronym 'SMART TIPS' stands for and an example for each.

S	**SPECIFIC**	_Example: Complete a SPECIFIC task (e.g. English Q.4, P.19)_
M	_____	_____
A	_____	_____
R	_____	_____
T	_____	_____
T	_____	_____
I	_____	_____
P	_____	_____
S	_____	_____

LESSON REVIEW

3-2-1

3 THINGS I LEARNED TODAY   _____

_____

_____

2 THINGS I WILL CHANGE/IMPROVE   _____

_____

1 THING I WANT TO KNOW MORE ABOUT   _____

TRAFFIC LIGHTS

COLOUR THE TRAFFIC LIGHT WHICH BEST REPRESENTS YOUR UNDERSTANDING IN TODAY'S LESSON

Red: I don't understand at all and need help

Orange: I need some support and don't fully understand some aspects of what we learned about

Green: I am happy that I understand this lesson very well

INDICATORS OF WELLBEING

TICK THE BOX TO SHOW THE INDICATORS OF WELLBEING YOU IDENTIFY IN TODAY'S LESSON

LEARNING GOALS

At the conclusion of this activity, I will be able to;

- Define the concept of 'meditation'
- Recognise the various types of meditation and identify benefits of meditating
- Practise a meditation session for beginners and reflect on how it has affected me

JOURNAL ACTIVITY: (A) BRAINDROPS

Use the raindrops to write down all the things you know about meditation.

JOURNAL ACTIVITY: (B) REFLECTION

How has today's introduction to meditation affected you? Write about your understanding of meditation, your thoughts and feelings about meditation and its effectiveness.

_____

_____

_____

_____

_____

_____

_____

_____

_____

LESSON REVIEW

3-2-1

3 THINGS I LEARNED TODAY   _____

_____

_____

2 THINGS I WILL CHANGE/IMPROVE   _____

_____

1 THING I WANT TO KNOW MORE ABOUT   _____

TRAFFIC LIGHTS

COLOUR THE TRAFFIC LIGHT WHICH BEST REPRESENTS YOUR UNDERSTANDING IN TODAY'S LESSON

Red: I don't understand at all and need help

Orange: I need some support and don't fully understand some aspects of what we learned about

Green: I am happy that I understand this lesson very well

INDICATORS OF WELLBEING

TICK THE BOX TO SHOW THE INDICATORS OF WELLBEING YOU IDENTIFY IN TODAY'S LESSON

LEARNING GOALS

At the conclusion of this activity, I will be able to;

- Recall the concept of 'meditation'
- Recall the various types of meditation and recognise the benefits of meditating
- Practise a meditation session and reflect on how it has affected me

JOURNAL ACTIVITY: (A) HOW DO YOU FEEL BEFORE MEDITATING?

Colour in the face that best represents how you feel right now, before meditating, in yellow. You may be feeling more than one emotion. Feel free to colour in more than one face!

JOURNAL ACTIVITY: (B) HOW DO YOU FEEL AFTER MEDITATING?

Having completed a meditation session, colour in the face that best represents how you feel now. You may be feeling more than one emotion. Feel free to colour in more than one face!

JOURNAL ACTIVITY: (C) REFLECTION

Have you coloured in different emotions before and after meditating? Why do you think this is?

_____

_____

_____

_____

_____

_____

_____

_____

LESSON REVIEW

3-2-1

3 THINGS I LEARNED TODAY   _____

_____

_____

2 THINGS I WILL CHANGE/IMPROVE   _____

_____

1 THING I WANT TO KNOW MORE ABOUT   _____

TRAFFIC LIGHTS

COLOUR THE TRAFFIC LIGHT WHICH BEST REPRESENTS YOUR UNDERSTANDING IN TODAY'S LESSON

Red: I don't understand at all and need help

Orange: I need some support and don't fully understand some aspects of what we learned about

Green: I am happy that I understand this lesson very well

INDICATORS OF WELLBEING

TICK THE BOX TO SHOW THE INDICATORS OF WELLBEING YOU IDENTIFY IN TODAY'S LESSON

LEARNING GOALS

At the conclusion of this activity, I will be able to;

- Identify a variety of options which can be considered for a Winter Festival within the school community
- Explore ideas and possibilities in order to organise an activity
- Share roles with classmates and take responsibility for various tasks

JOURNAL ACTIVITY: (A) BRAINDROPS

Use the raindrops to write down your ideas for a Winter Festival which the class will organise.

JOURNAL ACTIVITY: (B) PLANNING

Event planning & My Responsibilities			
Area in the school being used			
Day & time of event			
My tasks	To do	With	Due date
1			
2			
3			

LESSON REVIEW

3-2-1

3 THINGS I LEARNED TODAY _____

_____

_____

2 THINGS I WILL CHANGE/IMPROVE _____

_____

1 THING I WANT TO KNOW MORE ABOUT _____

TRAFFIC LIGHTS

COLOUR THE TRAFFIC LIGHT WHICH BEST REPRESENTS YOUR UNDERSTANDING IN TODAY'S LESSON

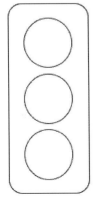

Red: I don't understand at all and need help

Orange: I need some support and don't fully understand some aspects of what we learned about

Green: I am happy that I understand this lesson very well

INDICATORS OF WELLBEING

TICK THE BOX TO SHOW THE INDICATORS OF WELLBEING YOU IDENTIFY IN TODAY'S LESSON

LESSON 30 - WINTER FESTIVAL EVENT (2) EXECUTION

LEARNING GOALS

At the conclusion of this activity, I will be able to;

- Complete assigned individual tasks effectively
- Execute a class project based on planning in previous lesson
- Reflect upon the experience of organising the Winter Festival event and learning in the lesson

JOURNAL ACTIVITY: (A) REFLECTION

1. What event did you and your peers plan to celebrate the Winter Festival Event?

_____

_____

_____

2. Describe what you were responsible for in preparing for this event.

_____

_____

_____

_____

3. Did you enjoy planning and running this event? Why?

_____

_____

_____

_____

_____

4. Who did you work with and what did you learn from them?

_____

_____

_____

_____

5. Do you feel the event was successful or unsuccessful? Why?

_____

_____

_____

_____

6. What did you learn about yourself from this event?

_____

_____

_____

_____

_____

7. What would you do differently if you were to plan an event like this in future?

_____

_____

_____

_____

_____

LESSON REVIEW

3-2-1

3 THINGS I LEARNED TODAY

_____

_____

_____

2 THINGS I WILL CHANGE/IMPROVE

_____

_____

1 THING I WANT TO KNOW MORE ABOUT

_____

TRAFFIC LIGHTS

COLOUR THE TRAFFIC LIGHT WHICH BEST REPRESENTS YOUR UNDERSTANDING IN TODAY'S LESSON

Red: I don't understand at all and need help

Orange: I need some support and don't fully understand some aspects of what we learned about

Green: I am happy that I understand this lesson very well

INDICATORS OF WELLBEING

TICK THE BOX TO SHOW THE INDICATORS OF WELLBEING YOU IDENTIFY IN TODAY'S LESSON

LESSON 31 - BEING ACTIVE (1) RELAY RACE   DATE _ _ _ _ _ _ _ _

LEARNING GOALS

At the conclusion of this activity, I will be able to;

- Discuss ideas and opinions with my class about what physical activity is
- Analyse how I feel before and after completing physical activity
- Complete a fun, active game with my classmates

JOURNAL ACTIVITY: (A) THINK, PAIR, SHARE

Jot down your thoughts and ideas around physical activity before sharing them with your classmates.

What comes to mind when you think about the term 'physical activity'?	← PHYSICAL ACTIVITY →	Is being physically active important? Why / why not?

_____

_____

_____

_____

_____

_____

_____

_____

_____

_____

_____

_____

JOURNAL ACTIVITY: (B) BEFORE AND AFTER, HOW DO YOU FEEL?

1. Colour the first column (Test 1) **before** the activity to record how you feel.
2. Following the activity, colour the second column (Test 2), using a different colour.

100									
75									
50									
25									
0									
	TEST 1	TEST 2	TEST 1	TEST 2	TEST 1	TEST 2	TEST 1	TEST 2	TEST 1	TEST 2
	HAPPY		LIVELY		SLEEPY		ACTIVE		ALERT	

LESSON REVIEW

3-2-1

3 THINGS I LEARNED TODAY

_____

_____

_____

2 THINGS I WILL CHANGE/IMPROVE

_____

_____

1 THING I WANT TO KNOW MORE ABOUT

_____

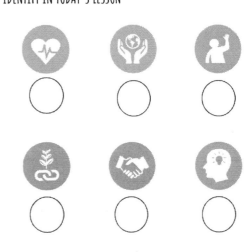

TRAFFIC LIGHTS

COLOUR THE TRAFFIC LIGHT WHICH BEST REPRESENTS YOUR UNDERSTANDING IN TODAY'S LESSON

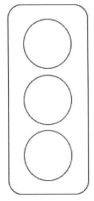

Red: I don't understand at all and need help

Orange: I need some support and don't fully understand some aspects of what we learned about

Green: I am happy that I understand this lesson very well

INDICATORS OF WELLBEING

TICK THE BOX TO SHOW THE INDICATORS OF WELLBEING YOU IDENTIFY IN TODAY'S LESSON

LESSON 32 - BEING ACTIVE (2) WHY PHYSICAL ACTIVITY?

DATE _ _ _ _ _ _ _ _ _

LEARNING GOALS

At the conclusion of this activity, I will be able to;

- Recognise the impact of physical activity on how I feel
- Identify effects of being physically active on the body
- Apply recommendations for increasing fitness to an activity I enjoy

JOURNAL ACTIVITY: (A) REFLECTION

In the previous lesson, you completed a physical activity and recorded how you felt before and after. Now, write about what you learned in lessons 31 and 32 and if you noticed any differences in how you felt before and after the activity.

_____

_____

_____

_____

_____

_____

_____

_____

_____

_____

_____

_____

_____

_____

_____

_____

_____

_____

_____

_____

_____

_____

JOURNAL ACTIVITY: (B) YOUTUBE CLIP

Complete questions 1-7 during, and after the clip.

1. What does MVPA stand for?_____
2. Name one benefit of physical activity? _____
3. What is the best exercise? _____
4. What is intensity? _____
5. What happens to your heart rate when you participate in vigorous intensity physical activity? _____
   _____
6. Give 3 examples of physical activities recommended in this video clip.
   _____
7. To improve your fitness, you are advised to increase frequency, duration and intensity. Give examples of how you could do this in an activity you enjoy.
   _____

LESSON REVIEW

3-2-1

3 THINGS I LEARNED TODAY

----

2 THINGS I WILL CHANGE/IMPROVE

----

1 THING I WANT TO KNOW MORE ABOUT

TRAFFIC LIGHTS

COLOUR THE TRAFFIC LIGHT WHICH BEST REPRESENTS YOUR UNDERSTANDING IN TODAY'S LESSON

Red: I don't understand at all and need help

Orange: I need some support and don't fully understand some aspects of what we learned about

Green: I am happy that I understand this lesson very well

INDICATORS OF WELLBEING

TICK THE BOX TO SHOW THE INDICATORS OF WELLBEING YOU IDENTIFY IN TODAY'S LESSON

LESSON 33 - OUR ENVIRONMENT (1)   DATE _____

LEARNING GOALS

At the conclusion of this activity, I will be able to;

- Identify all the things I can think of that are affecting the environment
- Recognise and become aware of issues relating to climate change
- Propose changes I would like to see in Ireland

JOURNAL ACTIVITY: (A) BRAIN DROPS

Use the raindrops to write down all the negative things you can think of that are affecting the environment.

JOURNAL ACTIVITY: (B) MY IDEAS

In Ireland, the Minister for Climate Action, Communication Networks and Transport takes responsibility for Climate Action.

1. What is his/her name? _____

2. If you could ask him/her one question or make one suggestion, what would it be? Write your ideas below.

LESSON REVIEW

3-2-1

3 THINGS I LEARNED TODAY _____

_____

_____

2 THINGS I WILL CHANGE/IMPROVE _____

_____

1 THING I WANT TO KNOW MORE ABOUT _____

TRAFFIC LIGHTS

COLOUR THE TRAFFIC LIGHT WHICH BEST REPRESENTS YOUR UNDERSTANDING IN TODAY'S LESSON

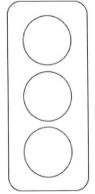

Red: I don't understand at all and need help

Orange: I need some support and don't fully understand some aspects of what we learned about

Green: I am happy that I understand this lesson very well

INDICATORS OF WELLBEING

TICK THE BOX TO SHOW THE INDICATORS OF WELLBEING YOU IDENTIFY IN TODAY'S LESSON

LESSON 34 - OUR ENVIRONMENT (2)   DATE _____

LEARNING GOALS

At the conclusion of this activity, I will be able to;

- Recall environmental issues identified in our previous lesson
- Recognise and become aware of issues relating to the use of plastic and disposal of plastic after it is used
- Propose changes I would like to make in school or at home to positively impact the environment around me

JOURNAL ACTIVITY: (A) BLUE SKY

- ✓ Blue Sky is an opportunity for you to use your imagination!
- ✓ Work with a partner and write all of your ideas for what we can do in school and/or at home to help the environment. Explore your ideas below.
- ✓ Don't be afraid to suggest or write down an idea. Even if it is incorrect, it may help someone else think outside the box too!

IDEAS: WHAT CAN WE DO TO HELP THE ENVIRONMENT?

Example:
- *Use a reusable water bottle instead of a plastic single-use one*

JOURNAL ACTIVITY: (B) MY FAVOURITE IDEAS

After exploring all the ideas with your class, write down your 3 favourite suggestions.

1. _____	2. _____	3. _____
_____	_____	_____
_____	_____	_____
_____	_____	_____
_____	_____	_____
_____	_____	_____
_____	_____	_____
_____	_____	_____
_____	_____	_____

LESSON REVIEW

3-2-1

3 THINGS I LEARNED TODAY

_____

_____

_____

2 THINGS I WILL CHANGE/IMPROVE

_____

_____

1 THING I WANT TO KNOW MORE ABOUT

_____

TRAFFIC LIGHTS

COLOUR THE TRAFFIC LIGHT WHICH BEST REPRESENTS YOUR UNDERSTANDING IN TODAY'S LESSON

Red: I don't understand at all and need help

Orange: I need some support and don't fully understand some aspects of what we learned about

Green: I am happy that I understand this lesson very well

INDICATORS OF WELLBEING

TICK THE BOX TO SHOW THE INDICATORS OF WELLBEING YOU IDENTIFY IN TODAY'S LESSON

LESSON 35 - RESILIENCE (1) WHAT IS RESILIENCE?

DATE _ _ _ _ _ _ _ _

LEARNING GOALS

At the conclusion of this activity, I will be able to;

- Recognise things I already do to support and nourish my resilience
- Identify and discuss additional things I could do to enhance my resilience
- Explore some potential choices which would harm my resilience

JOURNAL ACTIVITY: (A) DEFINITION

In your own words, explain what the term 'Resilience' means.

_____

_____

_____

_____

JOURNAL ACTIVITY: (B) QUESTIONS

1. What do you already do that supports and nourishes your resilience?

→ _____

→ _____

→ _____

→ _____

2. What additional things could you do to enhance your resilience?

→ _____

→ _____

→ _____

→ _____

3. When you are going through a tough time and feeling bad, what are some of the 'quick-fix' choices that you could make which - even though they make you feel good in the short-term - would actually harm your resilience in the long-term?

→ _____

→ _____

→ _____

→ _____

→ _____

JOURNAL ACTIVITY: (C) REFLECTION

Identify one challenge you have overcome in your life. Explain how you coped and 'bounced back' after it. It can be something big or small.

_____

_____

_____

_____

_____

_____

_____

_____

LESSON REVIEW

3-2-1

3 THINGS I LEARNED TODAY   _____

_____

_____

2 THINGS I WILL CHANGE/IMPROVE _____

_____

1 THING I WANT TO KNOW MORE ABOUT _____

TRAFFIC LIGHTS

COLOUR THE TRAFFIC LIGHT WHICH BEST REPRESENTS YOUR UNDERSTANDING IN TODAY'S LESSON

Red: I don't understand at all and need help

Orange: I need some support and don't fully understand some aspects of what we learned about

Green: I am happy that I understand this lesson very well

INDICATORS OF WELLBEING

TICK THE BOX TO SHOW THE INDICATORS OF WELLBEING YOU IDENTIFY IN TODAY'S LESSON

LESSON 36 - RESILIENCE (2) PROMOTING RESILIENCE

LEARNING GOALS

At the conclusion of this activity, I will be able to;

- Use selected key words / phrases from the previous lesson on resilience in badge format
- Design a badge to promote resilience
- Execute my design, creating a finished product

JOURNAL ACTIVITY: (A) PLAN YOUR RESILIENCE BADGE DESIGN

1. Look back at Lesson 35 and write some key words / phrases about resilience in the boxes below that you would like to use in your badge design.

2. What message do you want to get across in your badge design?

_____
_____
_____
_____
_____

3. How do you plan on getting this message across?

_____
_____
_____
_____
_____

4. What other important information do you want to convey?

_____
_____
_____
_____
_____

5. How will you reflect that in a visual image?

_____
_____
_____
_____
_____
_____
_____
_____
_____
_____
_____

LESSON REVIEW

3-2-1

3 THINGS I LEARNED TODAY

_____

_____

_____

2 THINGS I WILL CHANGE/IMPROVE

_____

_____

1 THING I WANT TO KNOW MORE ABOUT

_____

TRAFFIC LIGHTS

COLOUR THE TRAFFIC LIGHT WHICH BEST REPRESENTS YOUR UNDERSTANDING IN TODAY'S LESSON

Red: I don't understand at all and need help

Orange: I need some support and don't fully understand some aspects of what we learned about

Green: I am happy that I understand this lesson very well

INDICATORS OF WELLBEING

TICK THE BOX TO SHOW THE INDICATORS OF WELLBEING YOU IDENTIFY IN TODAY'S LESSON

LESSON 37 - SOCIAL MEDIA (1) RESILIENCE & SAFETY

LEARNING GOALS

At the conclusion of this activity, I will be able to;

- Identify some advantages and disadvantages of Social Media
- Reflect on my current level of online safety
- Discuss how Social Media can build or harm my resilience

JOURNAL ACTIVITY: (A) QUESTIONS

1. What's good about Social Media? List as many advantages as you can.

→ _____

→ _____

→ _____

→ _____

→ _____

→ _____

→ _____

2. What's bad about Social Media? List as many disadvantages as you can.

→ _____

→ _____

→ _____

→ _____

→ _____

→ _____

→ _____

→ _____

JOURNAL ACTIVITY: (B) DISCUSS & REPORT

1. What do you currently do to ensure your online safety? List 3 things.

a. _____

b. _____

c. _____

2. How can Social Media build your resilience? Give 3 examples.

a. _____

b. _____

c. _____

3. How can Social Media harm your resilience? Give 3 examples.

a. _____

b. _____

c. _____

LESSON REVIEW

3-2-1

3 THINGS I LEARNED TODAY

_____

_____

_____

2 THINGS I WILL CHANGE/IMPROVE

_____

_____

1 THING I WANT TO KNOW MORE ABOUT

_____

TRAFFIC LIGHTS

COLOUR THE TRAFFIC LIGHT WHICH BEST REPRESENTS YOUR UNDERSTANDING IN TODAY'S LESSON

Red: I don't understand at all and need help

Orange: I need some support and don't fully understand some aspects of what we learned about

Green: I am happy that I understand this lesson very well

INDICATORS OF WELLBEING

TICK THE BOX TO SHOW THE INDICATORS OF WELLBEING YOU IDENTIFY IN TODAY'S LESSON

LESSON 38 - SOCIAL MEDIA (2) THE NEED TO SWITCH OFF

DATE _____

LEARNING GOALS

At the conclusion of this activity, I will be able to;

- Explore some of the problems with social media / screen time
- Identify possible screen-free times
- Reflect on making possible changes to my own social media / screen time

JOURNAL ACTIVITY: (A) SOCIAL MEDIA / SCREEN TIME SCALE

Using the scale below, colour in the boxes to represent the number of hours that you spend on social media / screen time each day.

1 HR	2 HRS	3 HRS	4 HRS	5 HRS	6 HRS	7 HRS	8 HRS	9 HRS	10 HRS	11 HRS	12 HRS
13 HRS	14 HRS	15 HRS	16 HRS	17 HRS	18 HRS	19 HRS	20 HRS	21 HRS	22 HRS	23 HRS	24 HRS

JOURNAL ACTIVITY: (B) DISCUSS AND REPORT

1. What is the maximum time somebody should spend on social media / screen time each day? Explain.

_____

_____

_____

_____

_____

2. When should we 'unplug' from our screens? Give examples.

→ _____

→ _____

→ _____

→ _____

→ _____

→ _____

3. Are there areas in the house that should be screen-free zones? Give examples.

→ _____

→ _____

→ _____

→ _____

JOURNAL ACTIVITY: (C) REFLECTION

What real-life activities do you engage in that you enjoy? Briefly explain why you enjoy them. What real-life activities could you add into your evening to replace some of the time usually spent on social media / screen time?

_____
_____
_____
_____
_____
_____
_____
_____

LESSON REVIEW

3-2-1

3 THINGS I LEARNED TODAY

_ _

_ _

_ _

2 THINGS I WILL CHANGE/IMPROVE

_ _

_ _

1 THING I WANT TO KNOW MORE ABOUT

_ _

TRAFFIC LIGHTS

COLOUR THE TRAFFIC LIGHT WHICH BEST REPRESENTS YOUR UNDERSTANDING IN TODAY'S LESSON

Red: I don't understand at all and need help

Orange: I need some support and don't fully understand some aspects of what we learned about

Green: I am happy that I understand this lesson very well

INDICATORS OF WELLBEING

TICK THE BOX TO SHOW THE INDICATORS OF WELLBEING YOU IDENTIFY IN TODAY'S LESSON

LESSON 39 - MINDFUL COLOURING (1) WALLPAPER

LEARNING GOALS

At the conclusion of this activity, I will be able to;

- Define and interpret the term 'mindful colouring'
- Discuss the benefits of 'mindful colouring'
- Develop and arrange a 'mindful colouring' wallpaper

JOURNAL ACTIVITY: (A) REFLECTION

Having completed the mindful colouring activity, write about your thoughts and feelings about the creative process. e.g. Did you enjoy colouring in? Did you find it relaxing? Did you work well with your peers to create the wallpaper? What was the biggest challenge for you?

_____

_____

_____

_____

_____

_____

_____

_____

_____

_____

_____

_____

_____

_____

_____

_____

_____

_____

_____

_____

_____

_____

_____

_____

_____

_____

_____

_____

_____

_____

_____

LESSON REVIEW

3-2-1

3 THINGS I LEARNED TODAY

_____

_____

_____

2 THINGS I WILL CHANGE/IMPROVE

_____

_____

1 THING I WANT TO KNOW MORE ABOUT

_____

TRAFFIC LIGHTS

COLOUR THE TRAFFIC LIGHT WHICH BEST REPRESENTS YOUR
UNDERSTANDING IN TODAY'S LESSON

Red: I don't understand at all and need help

Orange: I need some support and don't fully understand some aspects of what we learned about

Green: I am happy that I understand this lesson very well

INDICATORS OF WELLBEING

TICK THE BOX TO SHOW THE INDICATORS OF WELLBEING YOU
IDENTIFY IN TODAY'S LESSON

LESSON 40 - SYNTHESISING INFORMATION (1) UNDERSTANDING THE CONCEPT   DATE _ _ _ _ _ _ _ _

LEARNING GOALS

At the conclusion of this activity, I will be able to;

- Define the process of synthesising information
- Give examples of various sources of information and examine how synthesising information can be applied to enrich my learning experience
- Practise the process of synthesising information

JOURNAL ACTIVITY: (A) QUESTIONS

1. In your own words, what does the term 'synthesising information' mean?

_____
_____
_____

2. List 7 sources / places you can obtain information from which would enhance your learning experience.

→ _____
→ _____
→ _____
→ _____
→ _____
→ _____
→ _____

3. List 3 times you could use synthesising information to enrich your learning experience.

→ _____
→ _____
→ _____

4. Can you recall 3 ways to successfully synthesise information?

(i)	(ii)	(iii)

JOURNAL ACTIVITY: (B) SYNTHESIS

Topic: _____

PREVIOUS BACKGROUND KNOWLEDGE	NEW INFORMATION FROM READING	FACTS LEARNED FROM DISCUSSION

LESSON REVIEW

3-2-1

3 THINGS I LEARNED TODAY

_____

_____

_____

2 THINGS I WILL CHANGE/IMPROVE

_____

_____

1 THING I WANT TO KNOW MORE ABOUT

_____

TRAFFIC LIGHTS

COLOUR THE TRAFFIC LIGHT WHICH BEST REPRESENTS YOUR UNDERSTANDING IN TODAY'S LESSON

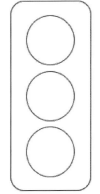

Red: I don't understand at all and need help

Orange: I need some support and don't fully understand some aspects of what we learned about

Green: I am happy that I understand this lesson very well

INDICATORS OF WELLBEING

TICK THE BOX TO SHOW THE INDICATORS OF WELLBEING YOU IDENTIFY IN TODAY'S LESSON

LESSON 41 - SYNTHESISING INFORMATION (2) APPLYING THE CONCEPT   DATE _ _ _ _ _ _ _ _ _

LEARNING GOALS

At the conclusion of this activity, I will be able to;

- Recall the process of synthesising information
- Recall examples of various sources of information which will enhance my learning and examine how synthesising information can be applied to enrich my learning experience
- Practise the process of synthesising information

JOURNAL ACTIVITY: (A) SYNTHESISING INFORMATION

Choose a subject and topic which you want to synthesise information from below.

SUBJECT & TOPIC	
PREVIOUS BACKGROUND KNOWLEDGE	
NEW INFORMATION FROM READING	

<table>
<tr><td>FACTS LEARNED
FROM DISCUSSION</td><td></td></tr>
</table>

LESSON REVIEW

3-2-1

3 THINGS I LEARNED TODAY   _____

                                  _____

                                  _____

2 THINGS I WILL CHANGE/IMPROVE   _____

                                  _____

1 THING I WANT TO KNOW MORE ABOUT _____

TRAFFIC LIGHTS

COLOUR THE TRAFFIC LIGHT WHICH BEST REPRESENTS YOUR
UNDERSTANDING IN TODAY'S LESSON

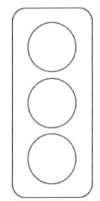

Red: I don't understand at all and need help

Orange: I need some support and don't fully understand some aspects of what we learned about

Green: I am happy that I understand this lesson very well

INDICATORS OF WELLBEING

TICK THE BOX TO SHOW THE INDICATORS OF WELLBEING YOU
IDENTIFY IN TODAY'S LESSON

DATE _____

LEARNING GOALS

At the conclusion of this activity, I will be able to;

- Identify vocabulary associated with having a healthy heart
- Give examples of activities and foods that contribute to a healthy heart
- Design a poster with my classmate to summarise what I have learned about having a healthy heart

JOURNAL ACTIVITY: (A) HEALTHY HEART WORD SEARCH

Find the 14 hidden words below as quickly as you can!

```
            Z L H N U                         U E E G V
          V V T L E S E                     M E P E J O L
        L T S L D S R E E N             J S R X X A D I W G
      A Q X Z O J E A L L O N         L M B U Z G F W I Y L N
      Q Z C O O A I W C T B R S     P N U E R E V U O S C P U
  U U I L N K T R D S G G A I P J H E P O F Y E S K W E L I Q
  Y H B R C U D E G U A J G T W D Z G A J B S I S P H H M I G
  B F F R G I T T B M S I A N E S M Y J I W G N G G Y G G S M
  Z K N T N R Y R J T B U J R O G Q X I V X X S B Y X W H C L
  A M C U F J H A I M A U E F R R E O N Q P X W C N Q F N D H
  G B Z Z X U T F B E R S I T H S T V J P C T R S O A F V Y B
  F X O B Z H L B L T N L H G C J J S K F M O H U C E D U Q T
  T H J P O P A A R J W T R V Q G Y I V C O V U T N Z C N Y A
    U B J I C E C B H U R S E C Q H J B L W M I H S L S V N
    A Y Y J K H U N V H M N V Y K Z X Z W I V W B G P P R V
      Z S Y K D B Z W O V F K R N H Q F M E N G C C R V L
        G A E J X W G E X D N R N R Q F I L F F J O N I
        K P Q H O N O S B X P K R N I E T O R P O I
          G J F K O V N A J G S C U S X A E K U Q
            T I U R F E N E T W E K I P I I O B
            C C T A A O U S P E M C J W F P
              A S C D R T D I P K A P H Z
              S S W V M Q A D W S G C
                B X Z R R O E M L N
                  N W E F E E J V
                    B H D L S B
                    P H X X
                      F N
```

ACTIVE	ARTERIES	NUTRIENTS	STRONG	BLOOD
HEALTHY	MUSCLE	FRUIT	VEINS	OXYGEN
PROTEIN	GAMES	VEGETABLES	DISEASE	

JOURNAL ACTIVITY: (B) A HEALTHY HEART

Watch the video and record the most important information to inform your poster.

LESSON REVIEW

3-2-1

3 THINGS I LEARNED TODAY

_____

_____

_____

2 THINGS I WILL CHANGE/IMPROVE

_____

_____

1 THING I WANT TO KNOW MORE ABOUT

_____

TRAFFIC LIGHTS

COLOUR THE TRAFFIC LIGHT WHICH BEST REPRESENTS YOUR UNDERSTANDING IN TODAY'S LESSON

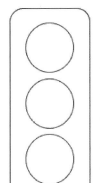

Red: I don't understand at all and need help

Orange: I need some support and don't fully understand some aspects of what we learned about

Green: I am happy that I understand this lesson very well

INDICATORS OF WELLBEING

TICK THE BOX TO SHOW THE INDICATORS OF WELLBEING YOU IDENTIFY IN TODAY'S LESSON

LEARNING GOALS

At the conclusion of this activity, I will be able to;

- Identify introvert and extrovert characteristics
- Demonstrate an understanding of the challenges introverts and extroverts face, as well as the contributions they make to society
- Establish my own position on the continuum

JOURNAL ACTIVITY: (A) DEFINITIONS

In your own words, explain what the following terms mean:

(i) Introvert

_____

_____

_____

(ii) Extrovert

_____

_____

_____

JOURNAL ACTIVITY: (B) QUESTIONS

1. Which do you think you are?

Introvert ☐   Extrovert ☐   Ambivert ☐

Give 3 reasons to support your choice.

→ _____

→ _____

→ _____

2. What situations in school would introverts find challenging?

→ _____

→ _____

→ _____

→ _____

3. Teachers often ask students to publicly present their work, sit in pods of desks and/or do group work. How can schools adapt to enable introverts and extroverts to flourish?

_____

_____

_____

_____

_____

_____

_____

_____

LESSON REVIEW

3-2-1

3 THINGS I LEARNED TODAY   _____

                                  _____

                                  _____

2 THINGS I WILL CHANGE/IMPROVE   _____

                                  _____

1 THING I WANT TO KNOW MORE ABOUT _____

TRAFFIC LIGHTS

COLOUR THE TRAFFIC LIGHT WHICH BEST REPRESENTS YOUR UNDERSTANDING IN TODAY'S LESSON

Red: I don't understand at all and need help

Orange: I need some support and don't fully understand some aspects of what we learned about

Green: I am happy that I understand this lesson very well

INDICATORS OF WELLBEING

TICK THE BOX TO SHOW THE INDICATORS OF WELLBEING YOU IDENTIFY IN TODAY'S LESSON

LESSON 44 - FILM STUDIES (1) 'INSIDE OUT'   DATE _ _ _ _ _ _ _ _ _

LEARNING GOALS

At the conclusion of this activity, I will be able to;

- Label different emotions which could be experienced as a teen
- Recognise and describe how these different emotions affect me both internally and externally
- Analyse the film 'Inside Out' and answer questions about the film

JOURNAL ACTIVITY: (A) INSIDE OUT FILM QUIZ

1. What's the main character's name?   _____

2. Which two emotions were formed first?   _____

3. Where is Riley from originally?   _____

4. Where does Riley move to?   _____

5. What sport does Riley play?   _____

6. What kind of pizza disgusts Riley?   _____

7. Name Riley's imaginary friend?   _____

8. Name three emotions you meet in the film. _____

    _____

9. What is Joy chasing when she's sucked out of headquarters?

    _____

    _____

10. Where are Joy and Sadness when they become two-dimensional?

    _____

    _____

11. What do the islands in Riley's mind represent?

    _____

    _____

12. What are Bing Bong's tears made of? _____

13. What does Sadness do to memories? _____

_____

_____

14. What next phase is Riley entering at the end of the film? _____

_____

15. What is created inside Riley's mind at the end of the film? _____

_____

LESSON REVIEW

3-2-1

3 THINGS I LEARNED TODAY   _

_ _

_ _

2 THINGS I WILL CHANGE/IMPROVE   _

_ _

1 THING I WANT TO KNOW MORE ABOUT   _

TRAFFIC LIGHTS

COLOUR THE TRAFFIC LIGHT WHICH BEST REPRESENTS YOUR UNDERSTANDING IN TODAY'S LESSON

Red: I don't understand at all and need help

Orange: I need some support and don't fully understand some aspects of what we learned about

Green: I am happy that I understand this lesson very well

INDICATORS OF WELLBEING

TICK THE BOX TO SHOW THE INDICATORS OF WELLBEING YOU IDENTIFY IN TODAY'S LESSON

LEARNING GOALS

At the conclusion of this activity, I will be able to;

- Recall the different emotions which could be experienced as a teen
- Recall and describe how these different emotions affect me both internally and externally
- Analyse the film 'Inside Out' and create a new character for the film

JOURNAL ACTIVITY: (A) CREATE A NEW CHARACTER FOR THE FILM 'INSIDE OUT'

1. Draw and colour in a new character (emotion) which you would introduce to the film 'Inside Out'. You must use annotation to name and describe the character in depth.

2. Explain the role the new character (emotion) would play in Riley's life and also in the film in general.

_____

_____

_____

_____

_____

_____

_____

_____

_____

LESSON REVIEW

3-2-1

3 THINGS I LEARNED TODAY   _

_ _

_ _

2 THINGS I WILL CHANGE/IMPROVE   _

_ _

1 THING I WANT TO KNOW MORE ABOUT   _

TRAFFIC LIGHTS

COLOUR THE TRAFFIC LIGHT WHICH BEST REPRESENTS YOUR UNDERSTANDING IN TODAY'S LESSON

Red: I don't understand at all and need help

Orange: I need some support and don't fully understand some aspects of what we learned about

Green: I am happy that I understand this lesson very well

INDICATORS OF WELLBEING

TICK THE BOX TO SHOW THE INDICATORS OF WELLBEING YOU IDENTIFY IN TODAY'S LESSON

LESSON 46 - WHAT TYPE OF LEARNER ARE YOU? (2)

LEARNING GOALS

At the conclusion of this activity, I will be able to;

- Recall different learning styles and traits of each type of learner
- Reflect upon my learning style(s) and use of learning strategies so far this year
- Evaluate what strategies were successful and if I need to make changes

JOURNAL ACTIVITY: (A) REFLECTION

1. What is your strongest learning style (kinaesthetic / visual / auditory)?

_____

_____

_____

2. Since you discovered your learning style(s), what learning strategies have you used?

_____

_____

_____

_____

3. How have you used these strategies to improve your school work, homework and revision?

_____

_____

_____

_____

_____

_____

4. What subject areas do you find it easiest to use these learning strategies in?

_____

_____

_____

_____

_____

_____

5. Are there any subjects you find it difficult to use your learning strategies in? Explain.

_____

_____

_____

_____

6. List a different strategy you will try out in the subject mentioned in question 5. How will this build and protect your wellbeing?

_____

_____

_____

_____

LESSON REVIEW

3-2-1

3 THINGS I LEARNED TODAY

_____

_____

_____

2 THINGS I WILL CHANGE/IMPROVE

_____

_____

1 THING I WANT TO KNOW MORE ABOUT

_____

TRAFFIC LIGHTS

COLOUR THE TRAFFIC LIGHT WHICH BEST REPRESENTS YOUR UNDERSTANDING IN TODAY'S LESSON

Red: I don't understand at all and need help

Orange: I need some support and don't fully understand some aspects of what we learned about

Green: I am happy that I understand this lesson very well

INDICATORS OF WELLBEING

TICK THE BOX TO SHOW THE INDICATORS OF WELLBEING YOU IDENTIFY IN TODAY'S LESSON

LEARNING GOALS

At the conclusion of this activity, I will be able to;

- Summarise features of my learning style(s) in a clear and concise way
- Organise what I have learned into a clear format to display to my peers on a poster
- Design a poster with a partner, featuring the most important aspects of my learning style(s)

JOURNAL ACTIVITY: (A) MY LEARNING STYLE

Answer the following questions to get you started. See lessons 24 and 46 to help you!

My strongest learning style is:	
Traits of students with this learning style include:	
Strategies I can use to help me learn include:	
How using my learning strategies builds and protects my wellbeing:	

JOURNAL ACTIVITY: (B) PLAN YOUR POSTER DESIGN

Use the space below to create a draft plan for your poster.

LESSON REVIEW

3-2-1

3 THINGS I LEARNED TODAY _____

_____

_____

2 THINGS I WILL CHANGE/IMPROVE _____

_____

1 THING I WANT TO KNOW MORE ABOUT _____

TRAFFIC LIGHTS

COLOUR THE TRAFFIC LIGHT WHICH BEST REPRESENTS YOUR UNDERSTANDING IN TODAY'S LESSON

Red: I don't understand at all and need help

Orange: I need some support and don't fully understand some aspects of what we learned about

Green: I am happy that I understand this lesson very well

INDICATORS OF WELLBEING

TICK THE BOX TO SHOW THE INDICATORS OF WELLBEING YOU IDENTIFY IN TODAY'S LESSON

LESSON 48 - GRATITUDE   DATE _ _ _ _ _ _ _ _ _

LEARNING GOALS

At the conclusion of this activity, I will be able to;

- Define the term 'gratitude'
- Give examples of people and things in my life which I am grateful for and examine how showing gratitude for them makes me feel
- Practise the process of keeping a Gratitude Journal

JOURNAL ACTIVITY: (A) MY GRATITUDE JOURNAL

What are some of the things you are grateful for? Complete the following:

1. List 7 people who have made your life a little happier today (or any day).

i. _____

ii. _____

iii. _____

iv. _____

v. _____

vi. _____

vii. _____

2. List 7 things you are grateful for today (big or small).

i. _____

ii. _____

iii. _____

iv. _____

v. _____

vi. _____

vii. _____

3. Something that made you smile today is _____

4. Something that you are good at doing is _____

5. Something that you are looking forward to is _____

6. Something that you treasure is _____

7. Something that made a positive difference in your life is

_____

_____

LESSON REVIEW

3-2-1

3 THINGS I LEARNED TODAY
_____

_____

_____

2 THINGS I WILL CHANGE/IMPROVE
_____

_____

1 THING I WANT TO KNOW MORE ABOUT
_____

TRAFFIC LIGHTS

COLOUR THE TRAFFIC LIGHT WHICH BEST REPRESENTS YOUR UNDERSTANDING IN TODAY'S LESSON

Red: I don't understand at all and need help

Orange: I need some support and don't fully understand some aspects of what we learned about

Green: I am happy that I understand this lesson very well

INDICATORS OF WELLBEING

TICK THE BOX TO SHOW THE INDICATORS OF WELLBEING YOU IDENTIFY IN TODAY'S LESSON

LESSON 49 – BEING ACTIVE (3) ELECTRIC CURRENT

DATE _____

LEARNING GOALS

At the conclusion of this activity, I will be able to;

- Recognise the impact of physical activity on how I feel
- Interpret a signal made by my teacher to trigger a response in a team game
- Analyse my participation in physical activity and self-assess my success in meeting physical activity guidelines

JOURNAL ACTIVITY: (A) QUICK RECAP

Brainstorm: What did you learn about physical activity in previous lessons? Share what you can remember in a class discussion.

1. Name all the benefits of physical activity you can think of.

_____

_____

2. What does MVPA stand for?

_____

_____

3. What is intensity?

_____

_____

4. What happens to your heart rate when you participate in intense and vigorous physical activity?

_____

_____

5. How much physical activity should teenagers be doing?

_____

_____

JOURNAL ACTIVITY: (B) REFLECTION

Write about your thoughts and feelings around physical activity in your daily life. Are you meeting physical activity guidelines? In what ways are you active and what activities do you enjoy the most?

_____

_____

_____

_____

_____

_____

_____

LESSON REVIEW

3-2-1

3 THINGS I LEARNED TODAY   _____

_____

_____

2 THINGS I WILL CHANGE/IMPROVE   _____

_____

1 THING I WANT TO KNOW MORE ABOUT   _____

TRAFFIC LIGHTS

COLOUR THE TRAFFIC LIGHT WHICH BEST REPRESENTS YOUR UNDERSTANDING IN TODAY'S LESSON

Red: I don't understand at all and need help

Orange: I need some support and don't fully understand some aspects of what we learned about

Green: I am happy that I understand this lesson very well

INDICATORS OF WELLBEING

TICK THE BOX TO SHOW THE INDICATORS OF WELLBEING YOU IDENTIFY IN TODAY'S LESSON

DATE _ _ _ _ _ _ _ _

LEARNING GOALS

At the conclusion of this activity, I will be able to;

- Recall the concept of 'meditation'
- Recall the various types of meditation and recognise the benefits of meditating
- Practise a meditation session and reflect on how it has affected me

JOURNAL ACTIVITY: (A) HOW DO YOU FEEL BEFORE MEDITATING?

Colour in, in yellow, the face that best represents how you feel right now, before meditating. You may be feeling more than one emotion. Feel free to colour in more than one face!

JOURNAL ACTIVITY: (B) HOW DO YOU FEEL AFTER MEDITATING?

Having completed a meditation session, colour in the face that best represents how you feel now. You may be feeling more than one emotion. Feel free to colour in more than one face!

JOURNAL ACTIVITY: (C) REFLECTION

Have you coloured in different emotions before and after meditating? Why do you think this is?

_____

_____

_____

_____

_____

_____

_____

_____

LESSON REVIEW

3-2-1

3 THINGS I LEARNED TODAY

_ _

_ _

_ _

2 THINGS I WILL CHANGE/IMPROVE

_ _

_ _

1 THING I WANT TO KNOW MORE ABOUT

_ _

TRAFFIC LIGHTS

COLOUR THE TRAFFIC LIGHT WHICH BEST REPRESENTS YOUR UNDERSTANDING IN TODAY'S LESSON

Red: I don't understand at all and need help

Orange: I need some support and don't fully understand some aspects of what we learned about

Green: I am happy that I understand this lesson very well

INDICATORS OF WELLBEING

TICK THE BOX TO SHOW THE INDICATORS OF WELLBEING YOU IDENTIFY IN TODAY'S LESSON

LESSON 51 - MEDITATION (4) REFLECTION   DATE _ _ _ _ _ _ _ _ _

LEARNING GOALS

At the conclusion of this activity, I will be able to;

- Recall the concept 'meditation'
- Recall the various types of meditation and recognise the benefits of meditating
- Practise a meditation session and reflect on how it has affected me

JOURNAL ACTIVITY: (A) MEDITATION

Below, explore and write about your thoughts on meditation. Once you have expressed these in your Student Journal, you will be asked to select one of these thoughts and write it on a post-it note to stick up onto a big class poster.

1. What do you think about meditation?

_____

_____

2. When is the best time to meditate?

_____

_____

3. Has it helped you to relax?

_____

_____

_____

_____

4. How does it make you feel?

_____

_____

_____

_____

5. Who could benefit from meditation?

_____

_____

JOURNAL ACTIVITY: (B) REFLECTION

Use this space to write about how meditation affected you today.

_____
_____
_____
_____
_____
_____
_____
_____
_____

LESSON REVIEW

3-2-1

3 THINGS I LEARNED TODAY   _____

_____

_____

2 THINGS I WILL CHANGE/IMPROVE   _____

_____

1 THING I WANT TO KNOW MORE ABOUT _____

TRAFFIC LIGHTS

COLOUR THE TRAFFIC LIGHT WHICH BEST REPRESENTS YOUR
UNDERSTANDING IN TODAY'S LESSON

Red: I don't understand at all and need help

Orange: I need some support and don't fully understand some aspects of what we learned about

Green: I am happy that I understand this lesson very well

INDICATORS OF WELLBEING

TICK THE BOX TO SHOW THE INDICATORS OF WELLBEING YOU
IDENTIFY IN TODAY'S LESSON

LESSON 52 - CREATE A COMMUNITY THEMED DECORATION (1) PREPARATION

DATE _ _ _ _ _ _ _ _ _

LEARNING GOALS

At the conclusion of this activity, I will be able to;

- Examine the meaning of the concept 'Community'
- Give positive examples of communities which I am part of
- Design and create a decoration which will be displayed in school in a community-themed display

JOURNAL ACTIVITY: (A) INDICATOR WHEEL

Using the Indicator Wheel below, write in one example of each of the 6 Wellbeing Indicators and where you have seen this in a community you are involved in.

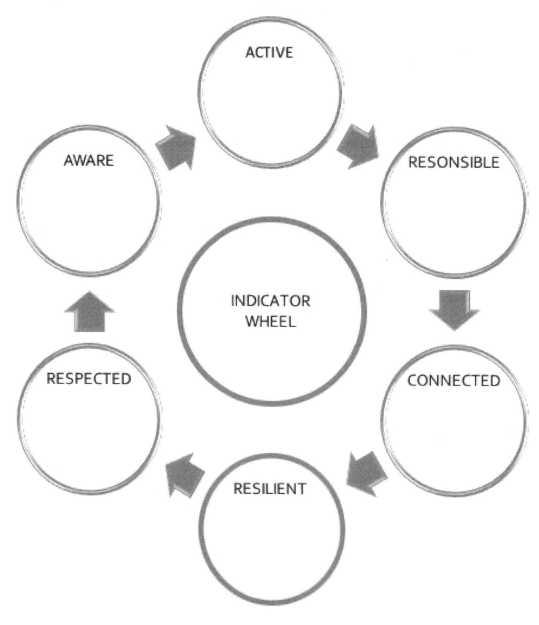

JOURNAL ACTIVITY: (B) PLAN YOUR DECORATION DESIGN

What positive people and communities will you draw / write about on your decoration?

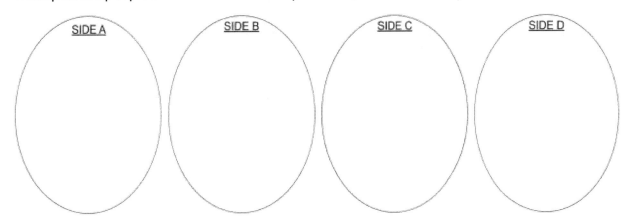

SIDE A   SIDE B   SIDE C   SIDE D

LESSON REVIEW

3-2-1

3 THINGS I LEARNED TODAY

_____

_____

_____

2 THINGS I WILL CHANGE/IMPROVE

_____

_____

1 THING I WANT TO KNOW MORE ABOUT

_____

TRAFFIC LIGHTS

COLOUR THE TRAFFIC LIGHT WHICH BEST REPRESENTS YOUR UNDERSTANDING IN TODAY'S LESSON

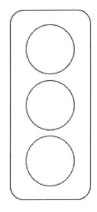

Red: I don't understand at all and need help

Orange: I need some support and don't fully understand some aspects of what we learned about

Green: I am happy that I understand this lesson very well

INDICATORS OF WELLBEING

TICK THE BOX TO SHOW THE INDICATORS OF WELLBEING YOU IDENTIFY IN TODAY'S LESSON

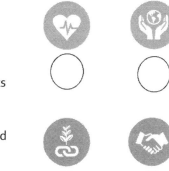

LEARNING GOALS

At the conclusion of this activity, I will be able to;

- Recall the meaning of the concept 'Community'
- Recall positive examples of communities in which I am part of
- Design and create a decoration which will be displayed in school in a community-themed display

JOURNAL ACTIVITY: (A) REFLECTION

Having completed the community-themed decoration and display, write about your thoughts and feelings about the creative process (e.g. Did you enjoy making it? Did you work well with your peers? What was the biggest challenge for you?)

_____

_____

_____

_____

_____

_____

_____

_____

_____

_____

_____

_____

_____

_____

_____

_____

_____

_____

_____

_____

_____

_____

_____

_____

_____

_____

_____

_____

_____

LESSON REVIEW

3-2-1

3 THINGS I LEARNED TODAY _____

_____

_____

2 THINGS I WILL CHANGE/IMPROVE _____

_____

1 THING I WANT TO KNOW MORE ABOUT _____

TRAFFIC LIGHTS

COLOUR THE TRAFFIC LIGHT WHICH BEST REPRESENTS YOUR UNDERSTANDING IN TODAY'S LESSON

Red: I don't understand at all and need help

Orange: I need some support and don't fully understand some aspects of what we learned about

Green: I am happy that I understand this lesson very well

INDICATORS OF WELLBEING

TICK THE BOX TO SHOW THE INDICATORS OF WELLBEING YOU IDENTIFY IN TODAY'S LESSON

LESSON 54 - TREASURE HUNT   DATE _ _ _ _ _ _ _ _

LEARNING GOALS

At the conclusion of this activity, I will be able to;

- Interpret 10 clues and successfully complete the treasure hunt
- Demonstrate teamwork to successfully complete the treasure hunt
- Analyse and assess my actions within today's task and how I contributed to my team successfully completing the treasure hunt

JOURNAL ACTIVITY: (A) REFLECTION

Complete the following 5 questions.

1. What role did you take on in your team? What did this involve?

    _____

    _____

    _____

    _____

2. Give one example of how you communicated positively with your teammates.

    _____

    _____

    _____

    _____

3. What did you find most difficult about the treasure hunt? Explain your answer.

    _____

    _____

    _____

    _____

    _____

4. What would you do differently to improve your team's performance?

    _____

    _____

    _____

    _____

5. What did you learn during the treasure hunt about how you work as part of a team?

_____
_____
_____
_____
_____
_____
_____
_____
_____
_____

LESSON REVIEW

3-2-1

3 THINGS I LEARNED TODAY

_____

_____

_____

2 THINGS I WILL CHANGE/IMPROVE

_____

_____

1 THING I WANT TO KNOW MORE ABOUT

_____

TRAFFIC LIGHTS

COLOUR THE TRAFFIC LIGHT WHICH BEST REPRESENTS YOUR UNDERSTANDING IN TODAY'S LESSON

Red: I don't understand at all and need help

Orange: I need some support and don't fully understand some aspects of what we learned about

Green: I am happy that I understand this lesson very well

INDICATORS OF WELLBEING

TICK THE BOX TO SHOW THE INDICATORS OF WELLBEING YOU IDENTIFY IN TODAY'S LESSON

LEARNING GOALS

At the conclusion of this activity, I will be able to;

- Explain the key elements of Junior Cycle Assessment
- Discuss my understanding of CBA and Examinations terminology
- Recognise and describe Language of Examinations

JOURNAL ACTIVITY: (A) WHAT DOES IT MEAN?

Draw a line from the word in the column on the left to the correct explanation in the column on the right.

Compare	Give reasons and evidence which supports an argument or point. Show why certain choices or decisions were made. Make sure you support your points with evidence.
Justify	Investigate or examine a subject. Provide a point of view after looking at both sides of an issue or question. Make sure you support your points with evidence.
Review	Look for similarities, but differences may be briefly mentioned, and come to a conclusion.
Discuss	Analyse the major points of the subject, step by step, and briefly comment on them.

JOURNAL ACTIVITY: (B) CBA DESCRIPTORS

What are the four descriptors used in the CBA grading system?

1. _____

2. _____

3. _____

4. _____

LESSON REVIEW

3-2-1

3 THINGS I LEARNED TODAY

_____

_____

_____

2 THINGS I WILL CHANGE/IMPROVE

_____

_____

1 THING I WANT TO KNOW MORE ABOUT

_____

TRAFFIC LIGHTS

COLOUR THE TRAFFIC LIGHT WHICH BEST REPRESENTS YOUR UNDERSTANDING IN TODAY'S LESSON

Red: I don't understand at all and need help

Orange: I need some support and don't fully understand some aspects of what we learned about

Green: I am happy that I understand this lesson very well

INDICATORS OF WELLBEING

TICK THE BOX TO SHOW THE INDICATORS OF WELLBEING YOU IDENTIFY IN TODAY'S LESSON

LESSON 56 - CBAS (2) HOW TO REFLECT　　　　　　DATE _____

LEARNING GOALS

At the conclusion of this activity, I will be able to;

- Identify ways in which I can reflect on my own learning
- Demonstrate use of reflection prompts and give examples of other tools of reflection
- Discuss and reflect on my own learning

JOURNAL ACTIVITY: (A) REFLECTION

In pairs, choose one assessment, project, experiment or task that you have completed recently in any subject and answer the following questions.

1.　What have you learned?

_____

_____

_____

_____

2.　What does this tell you about your strengths and areas you need to improve on?

_____

_____

_____

_____

3.　What do you need to do to improve your understanding / skills in this subject?

_____

_____

_____

_____

4. List three tools of reflection.

→ _____

→ _____

→ _____

5. Now on your own, use the **KWL** method to reflect on a different assessment or project you have completed recently. Again, this can be in any subject.

What do I now *Know*?	What am I still *Wondering* about?	What have I *Learned*?

LESSON REVIEW

3-2-1

3 THINGS I LEARNED TODAY

_____

_____

_____

2 THINGS I WILL CHANGE/IMPROVE

_____

_____

1 THING I WANT TO KNOW MORE ABOUT

_____

TRAFFIC LIGHTS

COLOUR THE TRAFFIC LIGHT WHICH BEST REPRESENTS YOUR UNDERSTANDING IN TODAY'S LESSON

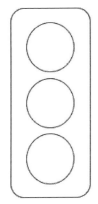

Red: I don't understand at all and need help

Orange: I need some support and don't fully understand some aspects of what we learned about

Green: I am happy that I understand this lesson very well

INDICATORS OF WELLBEING

TICK THE BOX TO SHOW THE INDICATORS OF WELLBEING YOU IDENTIFY IN TODAY'S LESSON

LESSON 57 - CBAs (3) THE SKILLS I NEED FOR CBAs

DATE _____

LEARNING GOALS

At the conclusion of this activity, I will be able to;

- Identify skills I already have, which will be useful when doing CBAs
- Name areas I think I might need help with
- Discuss what my classmates and I can do to manage our time while completing several CBAs in succession

JOURNAL ACTIVITY: (A) LISTING SKILLS

1. List the skills you already have which you feel will be useful when doing CBAs.

i. _____

ii. _____

iii. _____

iv. _____

v. _____

vi. _____

vii. _____

2. List other skills you feel you might need help to develop, which will also be useful when doing CBAs.

i. _____

ii. _____

iii. _____

iv. _____

v. _____

vi. _____

vii. _____

JOURNAL ACTIVITY: (B) DISCUSSION

What can you and your classmates do to successfully manage your time while completing several CBAs in succession? Give 5 examples.

i. _____

ii. _____

iii. _____

iv. _____

v. _____

LESSON REVIEW

3-2-1

3 THINGS I LEARNED TODAY

----

2 THINGS I WILL CHANGE/IMPROVE

----

1 THING I WANT TO KNOW MORE ABOUT

TRAFFIC LIGHTS

COLOUR THE TRAFFIC LIGHT WHICH BEST REPRESENTS YOUR UNDERSTANDING IN TODAY'S LESSON

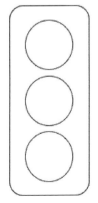

Red: I don't understand at all and need help

Orange: I need some support and don't fully understand some aspects of what we learned about

Green: I am happy that I understand this lesson very well

INDICATORS OF WELLBEING

TICK THE BOX TO SHOW THE INDICATORS OF WELLBEING YOU IDENTIFY IN TODAY'S LESSON

LESSON 58 - STUDY TIMETABLE (1) MY AFTER- SCHOOL / WEEKEND TIMETABLE   DATE _____

LEARNING GOALS

At the conclusion of this activity, I will be able to;

- Identify times for homework, after-school activities and leisure
- Apply my subject areas to a draft study timetable
- Create my own personal study timetable

JOURNAL ACTIVITY: (A) MY WEEKDAY ROUTINE

Answer the following questions:

1.	At what time do you travel to school in the morning? _____ At what time do you travel home after school? _____ What mode(s) of transport do you take to / from school? _____
2.	At what time do you usually have dinner? _____
3.	Record one of your **after-school** activities here: _____ _____
4.	At what time should you aim to go to bed each night? _____ At what time should you aim to relax before going to bed? _____
5.	Record your homework slots for Monday-Friday below: MONDAY: _____ TUESDAY: _____ WEDNESDAY: _____ THURSDAY: _____ FRIDAY: _____

JOURNAL ACTIVITY: (B) MY WEEKEND ROUTINE

Answer the following questions:

1.	Record one of your **weekend** activities here: _____ _____
2.	Record your typical **weekend** meal times here: BREAKFAST: _____ LUNCH: _____ DINNER: _____

LESSON REVIEW

3-2-1

3 THINGS I LEARNED TODAY

_____

_____

_____

2 THINGS I WILL CHANGE/IMPROVE

_____

_____

1 THING I WANT TO KNOW MORE ABOUT

_____

TRAFFIC LIGHTS

COLOUR THE TRAFFIC LIGHT WHICH BEST REPRESENTS YOUR UNDERSTANDING IN TODAY'S LESSON

Red: I don't understand at all and need help

Orange: I need some support and don't fully understand some aspects of what we learned about

Green: I am happy that I understand this lesson very well

INDICATORS OF WELLBEING

TICK THE BOX TO SHOW THE INDICATORS OF WELLBEING YOU IDENTIFY IN TODAY'S LESSON

DATE _ _ _ _ _ _ _ _

LEARNING GOALS

At the conclusion of this activity, I will be able to;

- Identify items to study for each of my subjects
- Discuss with my peers the appropriate topics to study for each of my subjects
- Record the appropriate topics to study for each of my subjects

JOURNAL ACTIVITY: (A) STUDY PLANNING

Use the grid below to record what you need to study for each of your subjects.

MATHS	ENGLISH	

LESSON REVIEW

3-2-1

3 THINGS I LEARNED TODAY

_____

_____

_____

2 THINGS I WILL CHANGE/IMPROVE

_____

_____

1 THING I WANT TO KNOW MORE ABOUT

_____

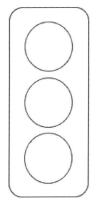

TRAFFIC LIGHTS

COLOUR THE TRAFFIC LIGHT WHICH BEST REPRESENTS YOUR UNDERSTANDING IN TODAY'S LESSON

Red: I don't understand at all and need help

Orange: I need some support and don't fully understand some aspects of what we learned about

Green: I am happy that I understand this lesson very well

INDICATORS OF WELLBEING

TICK THE BOX TO SHOW THE INDICATORS OF WELLBEING YOU IDENTIFY IN TODAY'S LESSON

LESSON 60 - HOUSE EXAMINATIONS / ASSESSMENT / RULES & GUIDELINES   DATE _____

LEARNING GOALS

At the conclusion of this activity, I will be able to;

- Predict some of the house exams/assessments rules for my school
- Interpret the reasons behind some of the house exams/assessments rules
- Compile a 'To-do List' for the night before each exam/assessment

JOURNAL ACTIVITY: (A) DISCUSS & ANSWER QUESTIONS

Discuss the question with your group / partner and compile and write your answer below.

1. Can you guess what some of our school's Exam / Assessment Rules are?

→ _____

→ _____

→ _____

→ _____

→ _____

→ _____

→ _____

→ _____

2. What should be on your 'To-do List' for the night before each Exam / Assessment?

→ _____

→ _____

→ _____

→ _____

→ _____

→ _____

→ _____

→ _____

→ _____

3. Choose 3 of the Exam / Assessment rules and explain the possible reasons behind them.

_____

_____

_____

_____

_____

_____

_____

_____

_____

LESSON REVIEW

3-2-1

3 THINGS I LEARNED TODAY

_____

_____

_____

2 THINGS I WILL CHANGE/IMPROVE

_____

_____

1 THING I WANT TO KNOW MORE ABOUT

_____

TRAFFIC LIGHTS

COLOUR THE TRAFFIC LIGHT WHICH BEST REPRESENTS YOUR UNDERSTANDING IN TODAY'S LESSON

Red: I don't understand at all and need help

Orange: I need some support and don't fully understand some aspects of what we learned about

Green: I am happy that I understand this lesson very well

INDICATORS OF WELLBEING

TICK THE BOX TO SHOW THE INDICATORS OF WELLBEING YOU IDENTIFY IN TODAY'S LESSON

LESSON 61 - POSITIVE SELF-ESTEEM (1) UNDERSTANDING

DATE _ _ _ _ _ _ _ _ _

LEARNING GOALS

At the conclusion of this activity, I will be able to;

- Define what self-esteem is and identify factors which influence self-esteem
- Recognise why positive self-esteem is important and deduce ways in which I can build positive self-esteem
- Practise giving and receiving positive compliments to peers to build positive self-esteem

JOURNAL ACTIVITY: (A) REFLECTION

Now you have completed the 'Positivity Page' activity, it is time to reflect on your actions by answering the questions below.

1. How did you feel writing positive comments about your peers?

_____

_____

_____

_____

_____

2. How did you feel reading positive comments that your peers wrote about you?

_____

_____

_____

_____

_____

3. Did you learn anything new about yourself?

_____

_____

_____

_____

_____

_____

4. What actions will you take to build your own positive self-esteem?

_____

_____

_____

_____

_____

_____

_____

_____

LESSON REVIEW

3-2-1

3 THINGS I LEARNED TODAY

_____

_____

_____

2 THINGS I WILL CHANGE/IMPROVE

_____

_____

1 THING I WANT TO KNOW MORE ABOUT

_____

TRAFFIC LIGHTS

COLOUR THE TRAFFIC LIGHT WHICH BEST REPRESENTS YOUR UNDERSTANDING IN TODAY'S LESSON

Red: I don't understand at all and need help

Orange: I need some support and don't fully understand some aspects of what we learned about

Green: I am happy that I understand this lesson very well

INDICATORS OF WELLBEING

TICK THE BOX TO SHOW THE INDICATORS OF WELLBEING YOU IDENTIFY IN TODAY'S LESSON

LESSON 62 - POSITIVE SELF-ESTEEM (2) MAINTAINING

DATE _ _ _ _ _ _ _ _ _

LEARNING GOALS

At the conclusion of this activity, I will be able to;

- Recall what self-esteem is and recall factors which influence self-esteem
- Recall why positive self-esteem is important and recall ways in which I can build positive self-esteem
- Identify realistic actions which will maintain my positive self-esteem

JOURNAL ACTIVITY: (A) DIAMOND 9

List 9 actions which you can take to maintain positive self-esteem.

1. _____

2. _____

3. _____

4. _____

5. _____

6. _____

7. _____

8. _____

9. _____

Now, using the 'Diamond 9' worksheet provided, prioritise these actions. The most important action is placed towards the top of the 'diamond' and the least important action towards the bottom. Actions of equal importance are placed on the same row.

JOURNAL ACTIVITY: (B) REFLECTION

WELL DONE! You have already explored, prioritised and shared actions you can take to maintain positive self-esteem.

Take time to reflect upon the following and write down how you feel about them.

1. How will you integrate these actions into your daily life?
2. Is there any aspect of your life that you feel could be improved by adopting and maintaining positive self-esteem?
3. Who can you ask for help to maintain positive self-esteem?

PERSONAL REFLECTION

LESSON REVIEW

3-2-1

3 THINGS I LEARNED TODAY

_____

_____

_____

2 THINGS I WILL CHANGE/IMPROVE

_____

_____

1 THING I WANT TO KNOW MORE ABOUT

_____

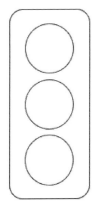

TRAFFIC LIGHTS

COLOUR THE TRAFFIC LIGHT WHICH BEST REPRESENTS YOUR UNDERSTANDING IN TODAY'S LESSON

Red: I don't understand at all and need help

Orange: I need some support and don't fully understand some aspects of what we learned about

Green: I am happy that I understand this lesson very well

INDICATORS OF WELLBEING

TICK THE BOX TO SHOW THE INDICATORS OF WELLBEING YOU IDENTIFY IN TODAY'S LESSON

LESSON 63 - MINDFUL COLOURING (2) WITH MUSIC

DATE _ _ _ _ _ _ _ _

LEARNING GOALS

At the conclusion of this activity, I will be able to;

- Recall and interpret the term 'mindful colouring' in my own words
- Recall the benefits of mindful colouring
- Construct and compose a mindful colouring page

JOURNAL ACTIVITY: (A) REFLECTION

Having completed the mindful colouring activity, write about your thoughts and feelings about the creative process, e.g. Did you enjoy colouring in? Did you find it relaxing? What positive / negative effect did the music have on you?

_____

_____

_____

_____

_____

_____

_____

_____

_____

_____

_____

_____

_____

_____

_____

_____

_____

_____

_____

_____

_____

_____

_____

_____

_____

_____

_____

_____

_____

LESSON REVIEW

3-2-1

3 THINGS I LEARNED TODAY

_____

_____

_____

2 THINGS I WILL CHANGE/IMPROVE

_____

_____

1 THING I WANT TO KNOW MORE ABOUT

_____

TRAFFIC LIGHTS

COLOUR THE TRAFFIC LIGHT WHICH BEST REPRESENTS YOUR UNDERSTANDING IN TODAY'S LESSON

Red: I don't understand at all and need help

Orange: I need some support and don't fully understand some aspects of what we learned about

Green: I am happy that I understand this lesson very well

INDICATORS OF WELLBEING

TICK THE BOX TO SHOW THE INDICATORS OF WELLBEING YOU IDENTIFY IN TODAY'S LESSON

LEARNING GOALS

At the conclusion of this activity, I will be able to;

- Design and construct a bridge using materials provided
- Evaluate my team performance, considering the criteria given for this challenge
- Reflect upon my learning using a reflective exercise in my Student Journal

JOURNAL ACTIVITY: (A) BRIDGE PLANNING

Use the space below to plan your bridge building with your team.

JOURNAL ACTIVITY: (B) REFLECTION

1. Were you happy with how you worked as a team in the bridge building challenge?

_____

2. Is there anything you would change if you were to complete this challenge again?

_____

3. Write about what you have learned this year in relation to teamwork and working with your peers.

_____

_____

LESSON REVIEW

3-2-1

3 THINGS I LEARNED TODAY   _____

_____

_____

2 THINGS I WILL CHANGE/IMPROVE   _____

_____

1 THING I WANT TO KNOW MORE ABOUT _____

TRAFFIC LIGHTS

COLOUR THE TRAFFIC LIGHT WHICH BEST REPRESENTS YOUR UNDERSTANDING IN TODAY'S LESSON

Red: I don't understand at all and need help

Orange: I need some support and don't fully understand some aspects of what we learned about

Green: I am happy that I understand this lesson very well

INDICATORS OF WELLBEING

TICK THE BOX TO SHOW THE INDICATORS OF WELLBEING YOU IDENTIFY IN TODAY'S LESSON

DATE _ _ _ _ _ _ _ _ _

LEARNING GOALS

At the conclusion of this activity, I will be able to;

- Compile a list of positive tips and advice for incoming 1st Year students
- Judge the list and recommend one of my best positive tips for incoming 1st Year students
- Compose a creative poster with my classmates, which will showcase the best positive tips and advice for incoming 1st Year students

JOURNAL ACTIVITY: (A) REFLECTION

Using the scale below, with 1 being very low and 10 being very high, colour in the boxes to answer the questions and then explain your answer in the box provided.

1. Did you enjoy working in pairs today to complete the Blue Sky Activity?

1	2	3	4	5	6	7	8	9	10

Explain your answer here:

2. Did you enjoy working on your own today to complete the Speech Bubble Worksheet?

1	2	3	4	5	6	7	8	9	10

Explain your answer here:

3. Did you enjoy working in a larger group today to complete the poster?

1	2	3	4	5	6	7	8	9	10

Explain your answer here:

LESSON REVIEW

3-2-1

3 THINGS I LEARNED TODAY

_____

_____

_____

2 THINGS I WILL CHANGE/IMPROVE

_____

_____

1 THING I WANT TO KNOW MORE ABOUT

_____

TRAFFIC LIGHTS

COLOUR THE TRAFFIC LIGHT WHICH BEST REPRESENTS YOUR UNDERSTANDING IN TODAY'S LESSON

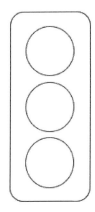

Red: I don't understand at all and need help

Orange: I need some support and don't fully understand some aspects of what we learned about

Green: I am happy that I understand this lesson very well

INDICATORS OF WELLBEING

TICK THE BOX TO SHOW THE INDICATORS OF WELLBEING YOU IDENTIFY IN TODAY'S LESSON

LEARNING GOALS

At the conclusion of this activity, I will be able to;

- Acknowledge ways I have changed since starting 1st Year
- Celebrate all my achievements, big and small, in 1st Year
- Reflect upon having successfully completed the 1st Year Nurture Wellbeing Programme

JOURNAL ACTIVITY: (A) REFLECTION

Having successfully completed the 1st Year Nurture Wellbeing Programme, write about which lesson(s) you feel contributed most to the development, care and nurturing of your own personal wellbeing.

_____

_____

_____

_____

_____

_____

_____

_____

_____

_____

_____

_____

_____

_____

_____

_____

_____

_____

_____

WELL DONE!
YOU HAVE SUCCESSFULLY COMPLETED THE
1ST YEAR NURTURE WELLBEING PROGRAMME!

LESSON REVIEW

3-2-1

3 THINGS I LEARNED TODAY

_____

_____

_____

2 THINGS I WILL CHANGE/IMPROVE

_____

_____

1 THING I WANT TO KNOW MORE ABOUT

_____

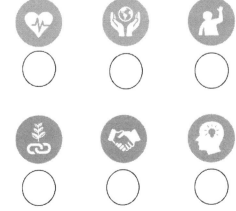

TRAFFIC LIGHTS

COLOUR THE TRAFFIC LIGHT WHICH BEST REPRESENTS YOUR UNDERSTANDING IN TODAY'S LESSON

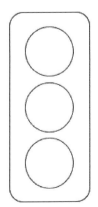

Red: I don't understand at all and need help

Orange: I need some support and don't fully understand some aspects of what we learned about

Green: I am happy that I understand this lesson very well

INDICATORS OF WELLBEING

TICK THE BOX TO SHOW THE INDICATORS OF WELLBEING YOU IDENTIFY IN TODAY'S LESSON

ADDITIONAL WRITING SPACE

ADDITIONAL WRITING SPACE

Printed in Great Britain
by Amazon